GW00871439

THE REBEL PUBLISHING HOUSE

Editing by Swami Anand Robin, M.A. (Oxon.)

Typing by Ma Anand Nayana
Ma Rashmi Bharti

Typesetting by Ma Premo, B.A.

Design by Swami Shivananda, M.F.A.

Paintings by Ma Anand Meera
(Kasué Hashimoto), B.F.A.
(Musashino Art University, Tokyo)

Production by Swami Prem Visarjan
Swami Paritosho, Swami Prem Prabodh

Printing by Mohndruck
Gütersloh, West Germany

Published by
The Rebel Publishing House GmbH
Cologne, West Germany

First Edition

ISBN 3-89338-045-0

In loving gratitude
to Bhagwan

Rajneesh Foundation Australia

Talks given to the
Rajneesh International University of Mysticism
in Gautama the Buddha Auditorium
Poona, India
from June 11 – 26, 1988

BHAGWAN
SHREE
RAJNEESH

ZEN:
THE QUANTUM LEAP
FROM MIND TO NO-MIND

Dedicated to the rainbows
as a symbol of total acceptance
of all colors of life

TABLE OF CONTENTS

INTRODUCTION

*...to dissolve like snow flakes
into the thin air of silence*

"Zen is a simple phenomenon – as simple as the taste of tea. But if you want to explain it, it becomes the most difficult thing in the world."

Bhagwan, as the ultimate 20th century Zen master, explains the inexplicable – delving his way into our understanding, alternating exquisite gentleness with a merciless sword. His own distinctive interplay of devices characterizes these talks: combining puzzles of ancient Zen anecdotes, earthy jokes, contemporary science, esoteric secrets and the Unexpected, He opens the gap from where a quantum leap can be made.

What is this leap and why do we need to make it?

The quantum leap, according to Bhagwan, is from mind to no-mind – from ego-mind to inner consciousness. It is all that is needed for self transformation and it can happen in the twinkling of an eye. No stopping half way: this is 100 % realization of our potential as human beings!

Bhagwan speaking on Zen is a must for anyone who senses "there must be more to life than this." There is more – and Bhagwan is infusing it into our reality, right here in front of our eyes.

Ma Deva Niseema, M.A.

NOTE TO THE READER

In April of 1988, Bhagwan introduced a new element into His daily discourses. For the first time in more than thirteen years, His audience had the opportunity to experience a specific meditation process in Bhagwan's presence, with His guidance.

Over a period of several weeks, the process evolved into its present form, and the text of each night's meditation is included in this book.

Each stage of the meditation is preceded by a signal from Bhagwan for a drumbeat, which is represented in the text by the following symbol.

The first stage is gibberish, which Bhagwan has described as "cleansing your mind of all kinds of dust...speaking any language that you *don't* know... throwing all your craziness out." For several moments, the hall goes completely mad, as thousands of people shout, scream, babble nonsense and wave their arms about.

The gibberish is represented in the text as follows.

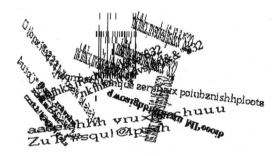

The second stage is a period of silent sitting, of gathering the energy within. Bhagwan often says a few words during this stage of the meditation, to help this process go deeper.

The third stage is let-go, where each person allows himself to fall to the floor "as if dead" – in Bhagwan's words, to "die to the world, die to the body, die to the mind, so only the eternal remains in you."

A final drumbeat signals the participants to "come back to life," collecting and re-membering the experience so that it can remain as an undercurrent, twenty-four hours a day.

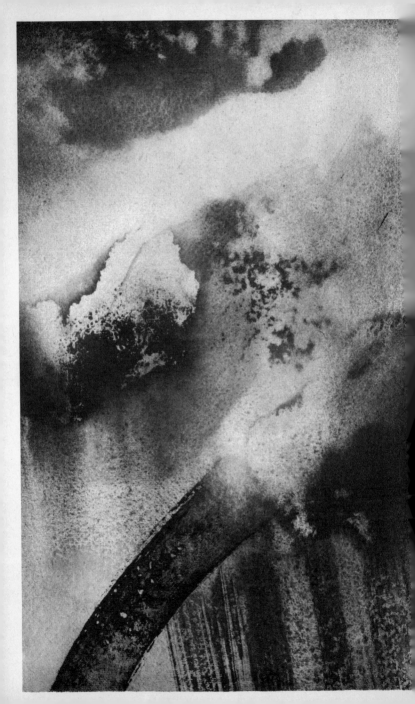

BABYSITTING
IS THE BASIC
BUSINESS
OF ALL BUDDHAS

Beloved Bhagwan,

The scholar, Ryō of Seizan, once had a meeting with Baso, who asked him,

"What sutra are you lecturing on?"

"The mind sutra," he replied.

Baso said, "By what do you lecture?"

Ryō answered, "With mind."

*Baso said, "The mind is like an actor,
the meaning like a jester,
the six senses like an acquaintance;
how can the mind lecture on a sutra?"*

*Ryō retorted, "If mind cannot lecture,
can't no-mind?"*

Baso replied, "Yes, no-mind can lecture all right."

Ryō dusted his sleeves and began to take his departure.

Baso called to him and said, "Professor!"

Ryō turned his head.

Baso said, "From birth to death, this is how it is."

Ryō had a great awakening and bowed in respect to Baso.

Baso said, "What on earth are you bowing for, nit-wit?"

*Ryō's whole body was now running with sweat.
Going back to his temple, Ryō said to the monks,
"I thought it could be said that all my life,
no one could lecture better than I on the sutras.
Today, a question by Baso dissolved the ice of a lifetime."*

Ryō gave up his lectures and retired far into the western mountains and was heard of no more.

...On another occasion Baso said to the assembled monks, "Believe that each and all of you have the mind which is the buddha! Daruma came from India to the middle kingdom to enlighten you with the truth he conveyed, of the Mahayana one mind."

A monk spoke up and said, "Why do you teach 'The mind is the buddha'?"

Baso said, "To stop the baby crying."

The monk said, "And when the baby stops crying?"

Baso said, "Mind is not the buddha."

The monk said, "Beside this, is there something more?"

Baso replied, "I will tell you, it is not some thing."

Maneesha, it is the beginning of a beginningless existential festival. Zen is festive, it is not scholarly. It condemns scholars as deeply as possible, because the scholar represents the defined mind, cultured mind, borrowed knowledge, dead scriptures. The scholar is a grave. Zen is a living rose of flowers. Nothing in it is dead, it is always and always. It goes on from beginningless to endless: characters change, leaves fall from the trees, new leaves start growing, the old ones disappear, the new ones arrive – it is a constant change. But in essence nothing changes – only on the periphery, only on the circumference, but never in the center. And the center is Zen.

I am happy to begin this series of talks with an anecdote about Baso. He is one of my beloved ones.

The scholar, Ryō of Seizan, once had a meeting with Baso, who asked him, "What sutra are you lecturing on?"

The poor scholar was not aware that he has entered into the den of a lion. Entering into it is easy, but getting out of it is impossible. Getting into the hands of Baso, you have already committed suicide. Baso was such a swordlike, sharp master. He killed people this way and that, and brought hundreds of people to enlightenment.

This poor scholar does not know that to meet Baso once is to meet your death. That's how the ancients have defined the function of a master. It is not to teach you, but to kill you: it is not to impart knowledge to you, but simply to take away all knowledge from you. Even the very sense of 'I' has to disappear.

The scholar was not aware that meeting Baso once is enough, twice will be too much. He asked him, *"What sutra are you lecturing on?"*

"The mind sutra."

Baso replied, *"By what do you lecture?"*

Ryō answered, "With mind."

Baso said, "The mind is like an actor, the meaning like a jester, the six senses like an acquaintance; how can the mind lecture on a sutra?"

Mind cannot speak, it can not even with a single finger indicate the ultimate. All that mind is doing is a controlled, relevant gibberish – on the surface looking very silent, inside a madhouse. This madhouse cannot say a single word about the truth; it knows nothing, although it plays the game as if it knows.

Ryō retorted, "If mind cannot lecture, can't no-mind?"

Just a logical, intellectual question, not authentic, not coming from his own experience... Because Baso says mind cannot speak on the truth, logically it can be asked, "Do you think then no-mind can speak?"

Baso replied, "Yes, no-mind can lecture all right."
Ryō dusted his sleeves and began to take his departure.
Baso called to him and said, "Professor!"
Ryō turned his head.
Baso said, "From birth to death, this is how it is."

The no-mind... Mind continuously changes: a child's mind is one thing, a young man's mind is another thing, a mature middle-aged mind is another thing, the mind of an old man is another thing. The mind is constantly accumulating, changing viewpoints, ideologies, religions. It is not very trustworthy, it cannot be relied upon. Today it may be a communist and tomorrow may turn against communism; today it may be atheist, tomorrow it may become a theist. Mind is just hot air, as polluted as Poona.

No-mind is your unpolluted nature, from the beginning to the end. Baso is saying, *"From birth to death, this is how it is."* No-mind is continuously singing its song whether you hear it or not; its music is there whether you hear it or not; its dance is there, though of course your eyes cannot see it. It is an eternal dance.

Ryō had a great awakening and bowed in respect to Baso.
Baso said, "What on earth are you bowing for, nit-wit?"
Ryō's whole body was now running with sweat.
Going back to his temple, Ryō said to the monks, "I thought it could be said that all my life

no one could lecture better than I on the sutras.
Today, a question by Baso dissolved the ice of a
lifetime." Ryō gave up his lectures and retired
far into the western mountains and was heard
of no more.

Meeting with a man like Baso is dangerous. It is not without reason that I am called the most dangerous man of this century. I am. Meeting me once, you will disappear, you will not be heard of anymore, you will not be seen again… One meeting is enough!

…On another occasion
Baso said to the assembled monks,
"Believe that each and all of you have the mind
which is the buddha! Bodhidharma came from
India to the middle kingdom to enlighten you
with the truth he conveyed of one mind,"
of this moment, of suchness.
A monk spoke up and said, "Why do you teach
'The mind is the buddha'?"
Baso said, "To stop the baby crying."

All the enlightened ones have been speaking, so that the baby does not start crying. Consoling, baby-sitting, is the basic business of all buddhas. The moment the baby grows, at the right time they are going to strike the baby. The real teaching will start only when you are mature enough, centered enough, receptive enough, aware enough. No buddha is going to waste a single hit. He will wait and console the baby, and once the baby is consoled the whole approach of the buddha changes. He does not speak in terms of the mind anymore. The mind is the most childish thing in the world. Once the master has helped you to detach your consciousness from your mind, the real teaching is very simple.

No-mind is the buddha.

Your ego is your immaturity.

Your egolessness is your awakening.
Just die to this moment deep enough
so that you can have a resurrection.

Then you will know that no-mind is the buddha.
And it has always been so. But to those who cannot
understand, the compassionate ones have been
saying to them that the mind is the buddha. It is just
out of compassion to keep you from crying,
because if you are not mature enough – and it is
said , "You are not at all; you are just a soap bub-
ble. Inside is nothingness and that is your nature" –
the retarded ones will be driven crazy.

The physician knows perfectly well in what
quantity the medicine has to be given, at what time
the disciple needs the ultimate hit so that he disappears, leaving behind him just a pure space.

Out of that pure space everything blossoms.
Into that pure space everything disappears.
That pure space is your being.
And *the monk said,*
"And when the baby stops crying?"
Baso said, "Mind is not the buddha."
The monk said, "Beside this,
is there something more?"
Baso replied, "I will tell you,
it is not some thing."

This no-mind, this pure silence is not a thing, it is
not some thing, it is the very life, the very consciousness, the very blissfulness, the eternal being.
It is not a thing.

Maneesha has asked,

Beloved Bhagwan,
The other evening I heard You say that intuition
and enlightenment are not different. Is that
because both are of no-mind? And does that

mean that when intuition is working within us,
we are having a small taste of enlightenment?

Maneesha, in your simple question you have raised many questions. First, the other evening never happened! The past is past. How many times do I have to remind you? There has been no other evening than this and there will be no other evening than this! Rather than being here, you are worried that you heard me say that "intuition and enlightenment are not different. Is that because both are no-mind?"

I want you all, not only Maneesha, to understand that this is not an assembly of philosophical, theological inquirers. This is a meeting of the buddhas. As far as your innermost self is concerned, you can give it any name, intuition… What does that word mean? It means 'knowing from within.' We understand perfectly what tuition means, what tutor means: knowledge coming from outside, a teacher, a tutor, a professor; all they are doing is tuition.

Intuition is that which arises within you, it is your very being. You can call it enlightenment. You can give it any name – it does not matter – names don't matter in this world of real existence.

And then finally you are asking, "And does that mean that when intuition is working within us…"

No, Maneesha, intuition is never working; it is simply there. What is working is always mind: what is always at rest, not working, is you. Your center is beyond working or not working, it simply is: it is a different language to understand – it does nothing. So when you think your intuition is working you are being befooled by your mind. Don't be befooled by the mind. Remember that intuition *is:* it does not work; it is a presence, an awareness. That's why I have called them two names of one experience: intuition, enlightenment, awakening, buddhahood – just names of the same unmoving center.

You cannot, Maneesha, have just a taste of it. Either you have it whole, or you don't have it. It is indivisible.

This gives me the chance to show you the meaning of individual. No dictionary, no encyclopedia will help. For them it will be very far fetched to connect individual with indivisibility, that which cannot be divided. If it cannot be divided, you cannot have a taste of it. You will either have to have it, or decide to remain in ignorance, but you cannot say, "I have got a little bit of enlightenment." That way it does not work.

You cannot say, "I am partially enlightened." Be – totally. And what name you give to that totality of your being is up to you. For the moment I have chosen the word enlightenment, because it has the quality of dispelling all darkness, misery, anguish, negativity; it brings you to your positive being, it brings to very heart, saying, "Yes," with every beat of the universe surrounding you.

But it is not, Maneesha, possible to have a partial experience. Just look at it this way: can you say to someone, "I am partially in love with you, just thirty percent. I will try a little more, but for the moment I am one third of my being in love with you"? If you say this to anybody he or she will think somebody has escaped from the madhouse! Even love cannot be divided, that's why love has always been taken as an example of enlightenment. The only thing that is similar in both is, they are indivisible.

But we are all living partial lives. Partially we love, obviously a very pseudo, very superficial, very unreal and false deception and nothing more. We are meditating partially. But nothing happens that way. Nature does not allow these great experiences in part. Nature is not America – you cannot have things on installment.

This American idea of installment is absolutely contrary to existence. Why not have it whole when it is available? You can cut *things* into pieces, but not *beings* into pieces. Beings will be dead if you cut them into pieces.

This is one of the most difficult problems for a scientific mind, because it is accustomed to dissecting. Only when something can be dissected will science accept its existence. And the consciousness of man cannot be dissected, hence science continues to deny there is any being, any immortal consciousness in man. It is really hilarious. Everything is in the lab of the scientist except the scientist himself; he is not there. He cannot accept that he is, unless he puts himself on the dissecting table, sees all the qualities, possibilities, inquires into every part, pulls them apart, joins them again and sees what happens.

Naturally if you cut a living being and then join it together again, you will have a corpse on your hands. Life will have disappeared.

It happened… Charles Darwin was celebrating his sixtieth birthday with his friends. And the children of his neighborhood…he was very friendly with children, with animals, with birds, with trees; it was his lifelong work to inquire into evolution, so he was interested in anything that grows; although he was an old man, he was very friendly with small children. All the children were wondering, "What should we bring him as a present on his birthday? His birthday is coming soon, and what can we present to a world famous scientist? There will be precious presents from every corner, what can we do? And he is such a great friend to us, something has to be done."

And they did something. They got hold of many insects, frogs, fish, grasshoppers – all kinds, whatever they could manage – and they cut them up to create a new being. The head was of a frog and the legs of a grasshopper. They were very happy that for the first time Charles Darwin would be surprised, because he had been working his whole life with insects, animals, their growth and evolution. "Let us see what he says about this insect."

The children came with their creation amongst the great scientists who had gathered to celebrate. They asked Charles Darwin, "Do you know this insect?"

Even Charles Darwin for a moment could not believe his eyes. He had roamed all over the world, finding all kinds of species, but he had never seen this…and these children of his neighborhood, where had they found it? He looked closely.

The children said, "Can you tell us the name?"

He said, "Yes, its name is hocus pocus."

Anything partial is going to be hocus pocus. Totality is the language to be learned here. To bring you to this moment, I try every device, because this moment is your no-mind.

The circus crowd is tense and silent, as Charlie the crocodile trainer cracks his whip. The crocodile opens its mouth…the crowd gasps as Charlie rolls up his sleeve and puts his arm inside the huge mouth. Charlie cracks his whip again and the croc shuts his mouth with terrific force, but stops an inch from Charlie's bare arm. The crowd is ecstatic.

Then the croc opens its huge mouth again, the white teeth glinting in the spotlights. This time, Charlie pulls out his prick and puts it in the croc's waiting mouth. There is deathly silence and Charlie cracks his whip. Quick as a flash, the croc shuts its mouth, but stops an inch from Charlie's prick. Then he picks up a huge wooden hammer and bangs it hard on the croc's head. But still he won't bite. Charlie takes a bow and then says, "Would anyone from the audience like to give it a try?"

A little old lady jumps up and runs into the ring. "Me! Me!" she cries. "But please, don't hit me so hard!"

Giovanni tells his friend, Zabriski, that he passed his American citizenship test by writing all the answers on the elastic of his underpants.

Zabriski borrows Giovanni's underpants and goes for the interview.

The examiner asks Zabriski the first question:

"How many states are there in America?"

Zabriski pretends that he is thinking. He turns around in his chair and sneaks a look inside the waistband of his pants.

"Thirty-four," he answers.

The examiner thinks that this poor man must be nervous, so he asks another question.

"What is the color of the American flag?"

Zabriski turns away and checks his shorts again.

"Green and purple," he replies.

The examiner decides to give him one last chance.

"Who was the first president of America?" he asks.

Zabriski looks over his shoulder, and stretches the elastic of his underpants. Then he looks up and proudly proclaims,

"Calvin Klein!"

Paddy walks into his local pub one evening and sees a smart traveling salesman leaning against the bar. He is impressed by the man's impeccable clothes, but what really catches his eye is the guy's beautiful red shoes.

So Paddy walks up to him and says, "I really love your shoes. What kind are they?"

"They are crocodile shoes," replies the salesman.

Paddy has never heard of crocodiles but not wanting to show his ignorance, he says, "Thanks," and then goes and asks Sam, the bartender, what a crocodile is.

"It is a big, ferocious animal that lives in the Amazon jungle in Brazil," replies Sam.

Paddy has fallen in love with those shoes, and when Paddy falls in love, he will stop at nothing. So, the next day, he sells his old Ford car and buys a ticket to Brazil. Two days later, he has hired a local guide and is paddling up the river in a small boat, in search of a crocodile.

A week later, and deep in the jungle, the guide suddenly shouts,

"Look! Mr. Murphy, a crocodile!"

Paddy grabs his huge knife and leaps into the river. A terrible fight follows, which is almost Paddy's last. But eventually, he kills the beast and drags it into the boat.

Exhausted, and bloody, Paddy triumphantly turns the crocodile onto his back, and then stares in amazement.

"Shit!" he cries, "it has got no shoes on!"

Now, the first step of meditation is throwing all your craziness out. It is a simple method, if you are not a coward – I mean if you are not a gentleman. It simply means gibberish. Speak any language that you don't know, or make sounds, but don't sit there like a buddha; that stage comes later.

Arup, first beat…

Go crazy!

Arup…

Everybody becomes silent, utterly silent.
Close your eyes and just be in.
Deeper and deeper, total and total…
Just be the buddha!
This is your very nature.

Arup, give the next beat…

Relax.
Relax so deeply…as if you are dead.
Let the body breathe, but you go on entering
deeper and deeper within yourself.

This is it.
No word can say it, no mind can explain it, but
it is deep inside you, already present.

Arup, give the beat…

Come out of your graves, back to life,
to resurrection,
fresh, silent, innocent.

Okay, Maneesha?
Yes, Bhagwan.
Can we celebrate now?
YES!

LISTEN TO
THE MESSAGE
OF THE RAIN

Beloved Bhagwan,

When Hyakujō was a young boy,
his mother took him to a temple, and entering,
she bowed to the Buddhist statue.

Pointing to the statue, Hyakujō asked
his mother, "What's that?"

"That's a buddha," she replied.

Hyakujō said, "He looks like a man.
I want to become a buddha afterwards."

Many years later, Hyakujō became a monk.
One day, as attendant to Baso,
he went wandering in the mountains.
On his return he suddenly began to weep.

One of his fellow monks said, "Are you thinking
of your father and mother?"

"No," said Hyakujō.

"Did somebody slander you?" asked the monk.

"No," answered Hyakujō.

"Then what are you weeping for?"
persisted the monk.

"Go and ask the master," said Hyakujō.

The monk went and asked Baso, who said,
"Go and ask Hyakujō."

The monk came back to the room and found
Hyakujō laughing.

"You were weeping a little while ago;
why are you laughing now?" he asked.

Hyakujō said, "I was weeping a little while ago,
and now I am laughing."

Maneesha, a few moments ago there was no rain and now it is raining. Existence is irrational. You don't ask the rains, "Why are you raining now when you were not raining a few minutes ago?" You don't ask the bamboos, "Why are you dancing with the rain, when you were standing like absolutely British gentlemen?"

Existence is irrational. The moment you ask why you have missed the point. This anecdote is great, great also in reference to your meditations.

When Hyakujō was a young boy,
his mother took him to a temple, and entering,
she bowed to the Buddhist statue.
Pointing to the statue, Hyakujō asked
his mother, "What's that?"
"That's a buddha," she replied.
Hyakujō said, "He looks like a man.
I want to become a buddha afterwards."

From a young man of twenty years, this is a great indication of a great future ahead. The stone statue of buddha cannot deceive him. At the most, it looks like a man. It is not a man: it does not breathe, it does not weep, it does not laugh. It is carved out of a stone; it is simply dead and will never laugh or cry or feel. How can it?

Hyakujō said rightly, "This certainly looks like a man; but I will not call it a buddha, because the very word 'buddha' means awareness and this stone is not aware. I want to become a buddha afterwards – not like a stone statue but a dancing, singing, laughing, alive buddha."

A buddha that cannot dance is not much of a buddha. A buddha is essential silence and being. If you can be silent this evening, the opportunity is great. The whole sky is pouring around you with a single indication: "Wake up, you have been asleep too long."

In this silence that awakening is possible. In this silence the stone buddha can start laughing, can start dancing, can start breathing. And remember, just as Hyakujō was not ready to worship a stone buddha, I am also against all worship.

The worshipper is the worshipped.

You don't have to worship anyone else.

Your innermost being is the highest and the most precious, the most existential and conscious point. There is nothing higher than it. You need not worship, you can only meditate.

Remember the difference between worship and meditation. The mother was saying, "Worship, pray!" and Hyakujō, a young man, was saying, "I want to be."

Prayer is always addressed to somebody else.

Prayer is not religious.

Worship is not religious.

Being fully aware and silent is the only way of knowing the taste of religion. This is a good opportunity.

The clouds come at the right time. Listen to the message of the rain. It simply is: just be like it. In a silent space, the dance of the rain, the whisper of the bamboos…and you have come home.

Many years later, Hyakujō became a monk.

One day, as attendant to Baso, – a great master, one of the greatest after Mahakashyapa –

he went wandering in the mountains.

On his return he suddenly began to weep.

Note the point, that he suddenly began to weep. There was no reason at all.

One of his fellow monks said, "Are you thinking of your father and mother?"

"No," said Hyakujō.

"Did somebody slander you?" asked the monk.

"No," answered Hyakujō.
"Then what are you weeping for?"
persisted the monk.

Why? That is the question mind goes on persist-
ing in. For the mind, everything has to be based on
a certain reason, a cause. Mind does not allow anything without reason, without causality. And because of this persistence, mind misses the most
essential question of your own being: why you are.

You can look here and there. Perhaps somebody
will tell you why you are. But nobody in the whole
history of consciousness has been able to say why
he is. All that you can do is shrug your shoulders: I
am, there is no question of why.

Hyakujō was right in telling the monk, *"Go and
ask the master."*
The monk went and asked Baso.
Baso said, "Go back and ask Hyakujō."
*The monk came back to the room and found
Hyakujō laughing.*

Now this is too much for the reasonable mind,
this is absurd… Now look, the rains are trying to
stop. This is not right. Just before they were at their
peak and now they are becoming silent to participate in your silence.

But there is no why. You cannot ask the bamboos; you cannot ask the roses; you cannot ask any
living being. Life simply is. Sometimes it weeps,
sometimes it laughs, and when it weeps without
any reason, weeping is a tremendous cleansing.
And when it laughs without reason, the laughing
reaches to a deeper point in your being. Like an
arrow it hits to the very heart of you and your existence.

The monk went and asked Baso, who said,
"Go and ask Hyakujō."

The monk came back to the room and found Hyakujō laughing.
"You were weeping a little while ago; why are you laughing now?"

The monk must have been a man of intellectual merit, a professor.

Hyakujō said, "I was weeping a little while ago and now I am laughing."

What is the problem? This is what Zen calls a quantum leap: from mind to no-mind; from reason to existence; from thinking to silence – a quantum leap. Mind cannot stop asking why. But your consciousness never asks why. The acceptance of consciousness and its trust in existence is absolute and uncategorical.

Have you ever asked why you are? You can ask about things...why a bicycle is or a car is. They have some utility. But what utility have you? Yes, you can rent a bicycle but that is not much of a utility. Somebody else would have done it. You cannot find a reason, wherever you search and search. The answer will be simply, "I am here without any reason." Why is irrelevant.

This I am calling the quantum leap. Meditation is nothing but a quantum leap from continuously asking questions into drowning yourself in a pure innocence where no question arises and no answer has to be given.

This is moment to moment living.
This is moment to moment loving.
This is the dance of the moment.

This small anecdote contains the very essence of Zen. If you can understand this small anecdote, you have understood all that is worth understanding.

Just be: it is your birthright.
There is no question of why.

You have been here all the time and you will be here all the time. It is a wrong conception when we say: Time passes by. The reality is that you, the witness, remain always the same, never old, never young, never child, never man, never woman – just a point of light which goes on from eternity to eternity. There is no reason to ask. And anyway, whom are you going to ask? Other than you who can answer why you are here? And you have not gone deep enough into yourself to find who you are. To ask the question, you have to find yourself first.

Those who have gone within themselves to find who is in have not returned back, because the further in they went, the more the ice melted; and when they reached to the innermost, they themselves were not there, only a pure space. And this pure space is the only scripture Zen will accept as holy. It is not man-made. It is not born. It knows nothing of death.

It simply goes on and on, flowering in many ways, forming many houses to live in, moving from house to house, from body to body, from one species into another species. But all this movement does not leave any trace of change in your authenticity.

Hyakujō was absolutely right when he said, "I was weeping a little while ago, you are right. And now I am laughing. And who knows what is going to happen after my laughter?"

It is the very essence of Zen when I say to you about our meditation: Don't ask why we have to go into gibberish. You have to go into gibberish because you have to go out of it. Your minds are full of gibberish and nothing else. Say everything that you ever wanted to say and have not been able to say because of civilization, education, culture, society. Here, nobody is listening: everybody is engaged in his own business.

Only a few idiots may be watching what is happening. Rather than participating they are observing a phenomenal thing. But they will not know the taste when – like after all this rain a coolness comes to you – after gibberish a silence penetrates your being. Gibberish is simply throwing away all garbage.

It is difficult to do it anywhere else because you will wonder what people are going to think. This is the place where nobody is thinking about you. It is your business what you are saying, what you are doing, laughing or crying or speaking Chinese without knowing it...and making gestures. Nobody has time. It is so short that everybody has to do his thing first.

When you are in gibberish, you are alone; everybody is alone, minding his own business. You don't interfere and ask anybody, "What are you doing? What are you saying? What language?" No language, no rationality...everybody is trying to throw out the craziness. Everybody is trying to get out of the mind, out of the why.

And once you are out of the mind, you are in.

To be in the mind is to be out of yourself.

To be out of the mind is to be in your own being.

Maneesha has asked a question. Before answering her question I have an apology to make to Rupesh. Nivedano has been beating the drum. Now that crazy guy has gone into Rajasthan in search of more rocks to make a bigger fountain and waterfall. He was very worried about what would happen to the drum. Who will drum?

I had to convince him, "Don't be worried. Whoever drums, I will continue to call Nivedano." He was immensely happy. But I had promised only for the last series, which has now ended. Poor Rupesh was beating the drum under the name of Nivedano.

Yesterday, the series changed: I thought, now it is time to call Rupesh. But somebody mistakenly wrote on my board the name Arup. I wondered for a moment, has Rupesh changed his name without even informing me? But there was no time. So I had to call Arup. And I could see, when Rupesh gave a beat to the drum, the anger. I am sorry, Rupesh. Those drums are not responsible for it. Some drum is responsible, but the drums you are beating are not responsible.

Today I will call Rupesh until this series ends. But please be kind to the drums.

Now, Maneesha's question:

Beloved Bhagwan,
I have just remembered that we are not human thinkings or human feelings – we are human beings. We are meant just to be, aren't we?
It is not a luxury that only some people can afford – it is really okay just to be, isn't it?

Maneesha, whether you know it or not, you cannot do anything else than just to be. There is no way of being anything else except what you are. A rose is a rose is a rose. And however it tries, it cannot become the lotus. And the same is true about the lotus. It cannot become the marigold.

Everybody has to be respectable and dignified in his own being. Your thinking is very superficial, the first layer, not essential…it can be changed; it changes continuously. Your feeling is also not very deep. It is a little deeper than thinking, but it can also change in a split second.

You know your thinking changes and your feelings change. But there must be something inside you that does not change. That is your being, the unchangeable. Remain rooted in the being, then slowly, slowly you start growing in a way totally different from how people grow ordinarily. When people become more knowledgeable, more learned, their thinking is growing. When people become more emotional, sentimental, their feeling is growing; but they themselves remain the same.

If you know your being and remain there without going astray, you will find a totally different kind of growing – not growing old, but growing up; not growing into something else but growing more and more into yourself, being more and more you. And this brings great blessings, immense ecstasies.

Before we enter into ourselves, a little outside evening walk will do.

The zoo has hit upon hard times, and as the animals die, the director can't afford to replace them…until he has a brilliant idea.

Sometime later, Kowalski is walking past the zoo, when he sees a sign, "Strong man wanted, apply within."

So he goes in and the director tells him, "Our star attraction, Gregory the gorilla, has died, and I want you to replace him. All you have to do is put on this gorilla suit, go out there and thump your chest and eat peanuts."

Kowalski starts work right away. Every day he thrills the crowd by jumping and thumping. But the climax of his act is when he climbs up a tree in his pen and throws peanuts at the lions next door, who get really mad and try to climb the fence.

Unfortunately, one afternoon Kowalski is up the

tree when the branch breaks and he falls into the lions' den. He jumps up and starts screaming and shouting for help, until one of the lions walks over to him growling and snarling, and then says out of the corner of his mouth, "Shut up, Kowalski, or we will all lose our jobs!"

Meditate over this. It is pure Zen. Everybody is hiding behind a coat: somebody behind a gorilla coat, somebody behind a lion coat; somebody is a mouse, henpecked of course... Come out! And just be. All these coats that you are wearing are not your being.

During their tour of Europe, Ronald and Nancy are visiting Ireland.

One day, Nancy Reagan makes a discreet visit to the office of doctor Rattle O'Bones.

"How may I help you?" asks the doctor graciously.

"Well," begins Nancy, hesitantly, "it is a delicate matter."

"Do not worry, Mrs. Reagan," says O'Bones. "You can be frank with me and I will be frank with you."

"Very well," says Nancy Reagan. "Since coming on this tour, with all the different foods, my stomach is always full of gas. And although the gas has no smell and makes no noise, I find it quite embarrassing. Whoops!" she says, smiling sheepishly, "there goes another one!"

The doctor tries to cover his nose discreetly. Then he pulls some pills from his desk drawer and scribbles furiously on his notepad.

"Here," he says to Nancy Reagan, "this is an appointment with a leading specialist, and these pills should help restore your sense of smell!"

Two old Virginia farmers meet on the street.

"Hey, Jed," says one, "I have got a mule, sick with distemper. What did you give yours when it had that?"

"I gave him turpentine," replies Jed.

A week later, they meet again and the first old farmer shouts, "Hey, Jed, I gave my mule some turpentine like you said, it killed him!"

"Funny," replies Jed, "it killed mine too!"

Luigi's wife has just died, and as the funeral party is leaving the graveyard, Luigi is making a terrible scene.

"What am I-a gonna do?" he cries, tearing at his hair. "What am I-a gonna do?"

"My son," says father Garibaldi, the priest, "I know you have suffered a terrible loss, but you will get over it in time." And he starts leading Luigi towards the exit.

"What am I-a gonna do?" sobs Luigi. "What am I-a gonna do?"

"Just try to control yourself," replies the priest. "Time will pass, you will get over your grief and maybe in a year or two, you will meet a young woman and get married again, and everything will be fine!"

"Sì, father, I know all that!" says Luigi, "but what am I-a gonna do tonight?"

Rupesh, tonight beat the drum.

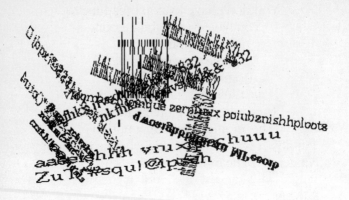

Rupesh…

Everybody become silent,
absolutely in.
Close your eyes, no movement,
just be still.
Feel the beauty of this moment.
Feel the freshness and the youth of this moment.
Feel the bliss and the dance
in the deepest core of your being.

Rupesh… The beat.

Everybody relaxes into death.
Let the body breathe, don't bother.

You don't have to stop breathing.
You have to stop being out;
be in.
And take the quantum leap
from mind into no-mind.
Feel the silent fragrance within.
This moment is a divine moment.
This moment you are a buddha.
Pin down your consciousness to this moment.
No head, no heart but just pure consciousness.

Rupesh…

You can come back to life,
to new life,
with new light,
with new joy,
with new eyes to see,
with new senses to feel,
with new intelligence to understand.

Okay, Maneesha?
Yes, Bhagwan.
Can we celebrate now?
YES!

A MASTER
IN YOUR OWN
RIGHT

(Just before Bhagwan's car comes,
a big black gorilla enters the hall
and sits behind Maneesha.)

Beloved Bhagwan,

After Hyakujō had become a master in his own
right, he asked Obaku where he had come from.

Obaku said, "From gathering mushrooms at the
foot of Mount Daiyu."

"Did you see the tiger there?" asked Hyakujō.

Obaku roared like a tiger. Hyakujō lifted up his
axe and made as if to chop him down.
Obaku gave Hyakujō a slap.

Hyakujō sang out and laughed, and went back
to his seat. To the monks he said,
"At the foot of Mount Daiyu there is a tiger
which you positively must see. Your old Hyakujō
has just had a word with him."

On another occasion, it was snowing,
and the monk in charge asked Hyakujō
to give a sermon.

Hyakujō said, "Falling in flakes, the color
scheme and pattern are complete. Why must I
go to the hall and preach?"

Life has never been taken with such ecstasy, joy
and bliss as Zen has done. The common religions
of the world, Hinduism or Christianity, Mohammed-
anism or Jainism, are all too serious. And their
seriousness keeps them imprisoned in words, in

theories, in philosophies. Their seriousness does not allow them to laugh, to sing, to dance, to be merry. They have spoiled the whole of humanity, they have destroyed the laughter of every child who has been born.

It seems there is something in laughter of which our so-called society is afraid. It is afraid, because laughter is going to expose its hypocrisy. Then you will see laughter everywhere, because hypocrisy is all around; but society has forced you to be insensitive to it.

Now look, just by the side of Maneesha, a gorilla is sitting. Gorilla, sir, will you stand up?

That's good.

Soon it is going to be very difficult, if tigers and gorillas hear you – and they are bound to hear, because here is a place where they can be respected.

After Hyakujō had become a master in his own right, he asked Obaku where he had come from. Obaku said, "From gathering mushrooms at the foot of Mount Daiyu."

"Did you see the tiger there?" asked Hyakujō. Obaku roared like a tiger. Hyakujō lifted up his axe and made as if to chop him down.

Obaku gave Hyakujō a slap.

Hyakujō sang out and laughed, and went back to his seat. To the monks he said,

"At the foot of Mount Daiyu there is a tiger which you positively must see. Your old Hyakujō has just had a word with him."

So playful, so childlike, so non-serious, so alive is the approach of Zen.

It is perfectly good for tigers and lions and deer to come to this gathering. They will appear, for this gorilla is going to spread the news. Gorilla sir, please be silent, although it is not your way, neither is it in your nature; but please don't start gossiping about this temple. We don't want tigers and lions, because we don't have space. Just wait a little... once we have got a bigger space, which we will be getting, then you can bring all the gorillas – you must have friends, a wife, children. A gorilla does not believe in celibacy, he is not a Catholic monk.

And having a few gorillas here dancing with you will be a real joy. Today you will have to be satisfied with only one. But when one comes, a second will be close behind him.

Just a few miles from here there is an ancient lake, Tadoba, deep in the forests. Its beauty is its deer, thousands of deer. You just have to be there at the time when the sun sets, when thousands of deer come to the lake to have a drink. The beauty is, as it becomes darker – you will be puzzled – their eyes shine like candles, as if thousands of candles are moving all around the lake, in a line.

I would love every species to be represented here, but unfortunately there is not much space and when such great people as gorillas start coming... They are your forefathers, be respectful. This is not me, but Charles Darwin speaking.

This story about Hyakujō, when he became a master in his own right... When one becomes a master in one's own right, when one dissolves, when one is no more, but just a pure energy, a space, nothing is written in this space – no scripture, no sermon...

There exists only one book in the whole of the world's literature which can be called religious. It belongs to the Sufi tradition; for a thousand years it has been given from master to successor. The first master who had it, Jalaluddin Rumi, has not been surpassed by any other Sufi. He is the only man who has been called *Mevlana* – Mevlana means master of masters. He had this book, though nobody knows from where he got it. But he would not show it to anybody; he would not take it out. He kept it hidden under his pillow and whenever he moved anywhere he kept the book with him. The disciples asked – and he had hundreds of disciples – "Why don't you say anything about this scripture?"

And he always said, "It is impossible to say anything about this scripture. Ask about anything, but not about this scripture; it is a religious scripture."

They said, "If it is a religious scripture, then it should be given to us, so that we can understand what religion is."

Rumi said, "You will get it only when I die. Wait."

When he became old and was on his deathbed, rather than being shocked that their master was dying, they were all curious: "As soon as he dies, we can take out the book from underneath his pillow. While he is alive, he won't allow it."

Rumi died. Nobody bothered about him; they rushed to take out the book, opened the book and got a greater shock than at Rumi's death: the book was empty. They turned every page – perhaps somewhere something is written – but from the beginning to the last – it must have been three hundred pages – it was empty, nothing was written in it. And Rumi used to say to them, "This is a religious scripture; perhaps this is the only religious scripture."

To become a master in your own right means to dissolve like snowflakes into the thin air of silence.

Still, a certain space will remain throbbing within you; that is your truth, that is your Zen. And to jump from your body, from your mind to that inner

space, unspoiled, untraveled, untrodden by anybody, you have taken the quantum leap. This quantum leap makes you a master in your own right.

Hyakujō asked Obaku where he had come from.
Obaku said, "From gathering mushrooms
at the foot of Mount Daiyu."

Zen has a special language. I have been insist-
ently reminding you not to take these words as
ordinary; they belong to a different kind of consciousness.

When Hyakujō asked, "Where are you coming
from?" he is asking, "Do you have a beginning?" If you
have a beginning, then you will have an end, they
come together. He is asking Obaku not about the
place he is coming from, but the space in which he is.

"Did you see the tiger there?" asked Hyakujō.
Obaku roared like a tiger.

I don't know whether this gorilla can give a good
gorilla shout.

(The gorilla screams loudly.)

Don't make Maneesha afraid! Be a gentleman! It
is a question of the dignity and respect of gorilla
culture. Anyway, everybody is happy that you have
come. I hope you will give a dance too at the end.
So get ready.

Obaku roared like a tiger. Hyakujō lifted up his
axe and made as if to chop him down.
Obaku gave Hyakujō a slap.

This is a strange dialogue, but both have recog-
nized each other, their mastership.

Hyakujō sang out and laughed. He has been
slapped by a stranger. Rather than replying, he went
out, sang and laughed *and went back to his seat.*

41

*To the monks he said, "At the foot of Mount Daiyu
there is a tiger which you positively must see.
Your old Hyakujō has just had a word with him."*

He informed his disciples that Obaku has also become a master in his own right: he has given the lion's roar.

*On another occasion, it was snowing, and the
monk in charge asked Hyakujō to give a sermon.
Hyakujō said, "Falling in flakes, the color
scheme and pattern are complete. Why must I
go to the hall and preach?"*

The falling snow,
the sound of it, the dance of it,
that peace that it brings
and the coolness that comes through it...
the sermon is going on!

Without any word these snowflakes are already saying it. What is the need for me to go to the seat and to give you a sermon? If you have eyes, ears, if you have your senses open, from every corner, from all directions the sermon is coming to you. You just have to be silent enough to feel it, to touch it, to taste it. It is not a word, certainly: it is an utterly living, dancing silence.

When Obaku slapped Hyakujō, do you see the response? If somebody slaps you, are you going to dance and laugh? If somebody slaps you, if you are strong enough, you will give him a good slap in return. And if you are the weaker one, you will turn tail and escape.

A Christian missionary was teaching. His whole teaching consisted of a few things in which this statement of Jesus was always present: "If somebody slaps you on one cheek, give him the other one too."

He had been preaching for years and the statement was clear. But one day a man stood up and slapped the missionary. For the first time the missionary was in trouble. He could not understand, "What kind of person is this?" But according to his own teaching he had to be consistent. So he gave him the other cheek, thinking he would be kind, but the man wanted to test the missionary to see whether he was preaching a truth of his own, or just something borrowed. He slapped harder.

Now the story turns completely upside down. The missionary jumped on the man and started beating him. The man said, "What are you doing? Have you forgotten your sermon?"

He said, "Jesus only talked about turning your cheek once. Now forget that, come on, man to man! To hell with Jesus! You have slapped me twice. I will kill you. That was only a sermon; you don't have to practice it; it's just a beautiful statement."

It was snowing, and the monk in charge asked Hyakujō to give a sermon.

In the first place Zen does not have any sermons; nor does it have any commandments, or discipline, or rules. It is a unique style of living so that you can come in contact with the divineness of existence itself.

Jews have ten commandments. Perhaps you know why there are ten. At that time, four thousand years ago, man used to count on his fingers. Ten is the ultimate figure, then there is repetition; for eleven and twelve, you are repeating another set of ten. You can go on repeating as many sets of ten as you want, but you cannot go beyond ten. Ten is the basic, because man learned arithmetic by counting on his fingers.

The story is that God created the world and went around asking the Babylonians, the Egyptians, the Arabs a single question, "Do you want a commandment?"

They all asked, "What is the commandment? Of course first we want to know what it is. In the dark we are not going to take anything."

And when he said, "Simple! Never, never look at another woman. Avoid all kinds of corruption."

The Babylonians said, "Then what else should we do? The whole joy of life will be gone. Keep your sermon to yourself."

The Egyptians did not ask, "What is the commandment?" They simply said, "Go ahead, find somebody else. Why should we listen to any sermon or any commandment? We are enough unto ourselves."

God was very sad; he has made these people and they are not ready to accept even a single sermon, a single commandment.

Finally he asked Moses, "Would you like to have a commandment?" And God forgot completely that a Jew responds differently from anybody else. Moses did not ask, "What is the commandment?" He asked, "How much does it cost?"

God said, "Absolutely free!"

Moses said, "Then why one? I will have ten!"

The poor Jews are carrying those ten commandments and from those ten commandments, Christians have borrowed, Mohammedans have borrowed... It seems there is some need in man that says to him that unless somebody else guides you, you will be lost. So he is always seeking guidance, without knowing the simple fact that in this world advice is the only thing which is given and never taken. You cannot become wise by asking wise people. The only way is to hear very closely the heartbeat of existence.

The poor Polack pope goes on kissing airports everywhere around the world. I would suggest to him that rather than kiss, please listen. Put your ears to the airport; that way perhaps you may hear something, but why taste it? Of course everywhere the taste is different. In India he tasted Hinduism for the first time when he tasted the cow dung. Stupid behavior! But it is thought he is very humble.

It is not true. Just a few days ago my secretary told me that he was in Brazil. The country is eighty percent Catholic, but that is all a formality.

In Greece I asked my sannyasins, "How many people are Greek Orthodox?"

They said, "Almost everybody is, ninety-two percent."

I asked, "How many people go to the church?"

They said, "Only four percent."

I said, "Are those four percent living or dead? Who are these four percent?"

They said, "Mostly old women, who have nothing else to do and the world wants to get rid of them."

It is only the priest who pays attention to them, because for that he gets his salary, that is his audience. He does not bother whether they hear or *can* hear; that is not important. He delivers the sermon; it is a profession.

But in these professions you will not find the truth. You will have to come closer to nature, not by touching airports, kissing airports. I have never read in any scripture that kissing airports is a religious duty. And this Polack pope thinks that this way he shows his humbleness.

Anando, my secretary, has brought the news that the Polack was very interested in Brazil, but very few people came to receive him at the airport. Where eighty percent of the people are Catholics, very few came to receive him. He was very angry. He asked the prime minister of Brazil, "What is the matter? Why has such a small group of people come?"

This is not humbleness…and he is wasting so much money. Each tour – and in a year he has three or four tours to different countries – each tour wastes eight million dollars, because people have to be brought to receive him. Everybody is in it as a business, "Unless you give a ten dollar note…." Because of this fellow, for the first time the Vatican is in debt; before him, it was the richest religion in the world. But thirty million dollars per year have to be wasted and what do you see? You see the pope kissing the earth.

This seems a totally new way to connect directly with God. When I say, "Be in touch," I don't mean start kissing the earth. I mean become more sensitive to everything the universe consists of.

Open all your doors, drop all your fears and paranoia and let existence come like a breeze dancing in you, laughing in you…and you will know what cannot be said.

Maneesha has asked:

Beloved Bhagwan,
Your voice is like a lifeline through the discourse, leading us into our gibberish insanity and then retrieving us, taking us into our stillness, being there in our death, and calling us back to resurrection and celebration.
I have heard it said that the master leaves the

disciple at some point and that ultimately one has to go by oneself. But you seem to be traveling with us into such intimate territory, walking so closely with us; and I have the feeling more and more that you are not leaving me, but meeting me.

Maneesha, you are right. You can leave me, but I will follow like a shadow.

Wherever you go I will haunt your heart.

I will come in your dreams.

I will meet you in different places.

Wherever five sannyasins are meditating together, the sixth...I will be present. It is a promise.

(There is loud laughter coming from outside Buddha Hall.)

This must be Sardar. After the meeting, Sardar Gurudayal Singh, you have to encounter the gorilla who is sitting behind Maneesha. In fact he should sit behind you! Don't provoke him, he can be dangerous.

But Sardar cannot resist...he laughs wholeheartedly, without bothering whether it is time for laughter or not.

Now, for Sardar Gurudayal Singh and for our guest, the gorilla, if he can understand... If he cannot understand, at least he can understand your laughter.

Captain Fearless, the infamous pirate, is standing on the deck of his ship, 'The Dirty Doc' – that is the name of the ship. When the lookout calls, "Italian merchant ship ahead!" Fearless calls his cabin boy and says, "Bring me my red coat, we are going into battle." Soon the Italian ship is overpowered and that night there is a feast of spaghetti and garlic.

The next day Captain Fearless hears the cry, "Three German merchant ships ahead!" Fearless calls for the cabin boy. "Bring me my red coat," he cries, "we are going into battle."

Soon the German ships are captured and that night during a feast of beer and sausage the cabin boy asks, "Excuse me, Captain Fearless, sir, but why do you always ask for your red coat before battle?"

"In case I am wounded," cries Fearless. "Then my men won't see the blood and become disappointed or disheartened."

The next day the lookout cries, "A fleet of English warships ahead."

Fearless turns to the cabin boy and whispers, "Bring me my brown pants."

Sidney and Sadie have had a lovers' quarrel and they have not seen each other for two days.

Sadie is sitting moodily, staring out of the window when the phone rings. It is Sidney.

"I am coming over to your house tonight," he says.

"Oh no you are not!" snaps Sadie.

"And I am going to throw you on the bed," Sidney announces.

"Oh no you are not," says Sadie.

"And I am going to tear off your clothes," says Sidney, "and make love to you!"

"Oh no you are not!" says Sadie.

"And," says Sidney, "I am not even going to wear a condom!"

"Oh yes you are," says Sadie.

It is raining one afternoon, so Virgil, the ventriloquist, goes into a bar. As he opens the door a stray dog pushes past him, nearly knocking him over, and then it goes to sit down near the bar.

Virgil sits on a bar stool near the dog and orders a drink. When he is served, Virgil looks at the dog and then asks the bartender if he is interested in buying a talking dog for five hundred dollars.

The bartender laughs at the idea, but then the dog says, "Please mister, please buy me. This man is so mean to me, he doesn't look after me and never feeds me!"

The bartender is shocked. "Did you say you wanted five hundred dollars for him?" he says. "Why do you want to sell him?"

I hate liars," replied Virgil, taking a drink.

The bartender hands over five hundred dollars and Virgil gets up and goes towards the door. "So long, you ungrateful creature," he says to the dog.

The dog looks up, "Ungrateful, is it?" says the dog. "Well, just for that, I am never going to speak again!"

Rupesh, give the first drum…

Rupesh...

Be silent, close your eyes
and gather your whole being in.
This is the quantum leap,
from mind to no-mind.
This space is you
and *this* moment is your only time.
In these two words
'here' and 'now',
the whole of religion is complete.

Rupesh, give the drum...

You fall dead.
Utterly dead.
I am not telling you to stop your breathing;
your body can go on breathing.
You be in,
deeper and deeper in!

Rupesh, the last drum…

Everybody has to come back to life.
This is resurrection!

One special beat for the guest gorilla.

No, Rupesh! Gorilla cannot understand it, do it *totally!*

(Rupesh gives a really good drumbeat and the gorilla shouts with joy.)

Okay, Maneesha?
Yes, Bhagwan.
Can we celebrate now?
YES!

(After the ecstatic Yaa-Hoo celebration, the gorilla starts dancing with Maneesha and after a while Sardar, coming from outside, joins the dance.)

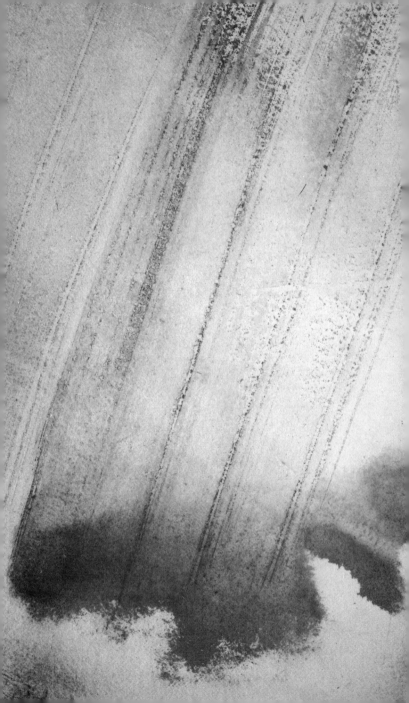

ZEN
IS AS SIMPLE
AS THE TASTE
OF TEA

Beloved Bhagwan,

Ryūge was asked by a monk, "What is the meaning of Bodhidharma coming from the West?"

Ryūge said, "Wait till the stone turtle speaks words of explanation and I will tell you."

The monk said, "The stone turtle has spoken!"

Ryūge said, "What did it say to you?"

The monk was silent.

One of Daibai's monks asked his master the same question, to which Daibai replied, "His coming has no meaning."

The monk brought this question up to Enkan, who said, "Two dead men in one coffin."

Gensha, hearing of this, said, "Enkan is a clever chap."

The same question – the meaning of Bodhidharma coming from the West – was brought to Sekitō, or "Stonehead", as he was also known.

"Go and ask the outside post of the hall!" he exclaimed.

The monk said, "I don't know what you mean."

"Nor do I," said Sekitō.

When Suiyrō put the question to his master, Baso, Baso kicked him in the chest and knocked him down. Suiyrō was enlightened. He stood up and, clapping his hands and laughing aloud, said, "A miracle! A miracle! The hundred samadhis and the countless mysterious truths are profoundly known to me now in the tip of one hair."

He made his bows and departed.

Maneesha, Zen is a simple phenomenon – as simple as the taste of tea. But if you want to explain it, it becomes the most difficult thing in the world.

These anecdotes indicate again and again the existential status of Zen, not philosophical, not theological. It is more poetry than religion, more music than philosophy; a language that is understood even by the bamboos, by the flowers, even by the cuckoos. It is a language of existence itself. This is the way existence opens its doors.

Mind is the enemy. The more knowledgeable the more dangerous, the more knowledgeable the more closed. When there is no-mind even for a single moment, you have come home: a thousand miles journey is finished in a single moment.

The questions asked are very symbolic. There are only a few questions that have been asked down the ages. Everybody knows the answer. Even the questioner knows the answer – as far as mind is concerned. But he is asking the question so that he can see beyond the mind and beyond the answer of the mind into reality itself.

Ryūge was asked by a monk, "What is the meaning of Bodhidharma coming from the West?"

This is one of the most important questions asked in the Zen tradition. Obviously, Bodhidharma is the most important master, who introduced Zen from India into China. The question: "What is the meaning of Bodhidharma coming from the West?" ...you will have to understand that the West does not mean what you know as the West. From China, the place Bodhidharma landed, India is West. The concepts of east and west are very relative. What is east from one point is west from another point: in itself, it is neither east nor west.

Where you are, inside – in the East or in the West

– there are no directions, no indications, just a pure isness. You are…and so strongly that you don't have to believe in it: you cannot disbelieve. All the religions of the world have been telling people to believe; and I want to make it clear to you that unless you come to a point where you cannot disbelieve, all your beliefs are meaningless. That point where you cannot disbelieve, that indubitable point, is neither East nor West.

That was the purpose of Bodhidharma going from India to China. When Bodhidharma reached China, they were strongly influenced by the thoughts and philosophy of Confucius and Mencius, both great intellectuals. But neither of them had known the peace of no-mind. They knew much and yet – they knew nothing.

Bodhidharma's master had sent him on this long journey. Three years he had to waste to reach China. He himself was a son of a king. His master gave him orders: "It is now absolutely essential that you should carry the message of *being in* to China, because it is being overwhelmed by Confucius, Mencius and other thinkers. They think they have found the truth. Go and make it clear that 'Mind is absolutely impotent. If you want to know the truth, you will have to have the courage to leave the mind aside. Push it aside and enter into your silence.' "

That was why Bodhidharma went to China. Obviously, it became a traditional question for every Zen student.

Ryūge was asked by a monk,
"What is the meaning of Bodhidharma
coming from the West?"
Ryūge said, "Wait till the stone turtle speaks
words of explanation and I will tell you."
Ryūge's temple was famous. He had a great turtle

in front of his temple, cut out of a huge stone.

He said, *"Wait till the stone turtle speaks words of explanation and I will tell you."*

He is saying, "This is not a question to be asked. And if you insist, I give you time. Wait till the stone turtle starts speaking." Obviously it is absurd: that stone turtle is never going to give any explanations.

But Ryūge has answered in the Zen way, in the Zen language. "Wait" is the secret word. If you can wait silently, the meaning will shower on you like flowers. Or the meaning will arise in you like a flame. But wait!

Our minds are in such a hurry. We have completely forgotten the beauty of waiting. We want everything to happen quickly. But nobody considers that waiting has a beauty which you miss when you are running after shadows.

Ryūge's answer was perfectly right, "Wait till eternity. But wait; and you will find the meaning of Bodhidharma coming to China. The meaning will not be told to you by somebody else. It will arise in your own being. Just be silent."

The monk said, "The stone turtle has spoken!"

These dialogues are immensely beautiful, a totally different play than Socratic dialogues or Martin Luther's dialogue. The monk thought himself competent enough to answer the question he himself has raised.

But you cannot deceive a master.

The monk said, "The stone turtle has spoken!"

Now, if Ryūge had been just a teacher, he would have been embarrassed to continue. But Ryūge was an authentic master.

Ryūge said, "What did it say to you?"
The monk was silent.

Now he found that he was not competent enough

to have a dialogue with a master, with an enlightened person...and he could not deceive. And anyway, you are only deceiving yourself.

*One of Daibai's monks asked his master the
same question, to which Daibai replied,
"His coming has no meaning."*

The question is the same. The masters are different. The answers apparently are different, but not truly.

Daibai said, *"His coming has no meaning."*

Meaning is always part of the mind. Without mind, there is no meaning, there is only silence. There is significance, there is beauty, there is dance, there is music, but no meaning. Mind is meaning: no-mind is no meaning. One of the names of Gautam Buddha is *tathagata*. It has many connotations. One of them is worth remembering at this point. It means, "Came thus, gone thus" – just like a breeze. You don't ask, "What is the meaning of the breeze coming and then going away?" You know the breeze has no-mind, hence you cannot ask the question.

Daibai said, *"His coming has no meaning."*

But remember the word 'no' because that 'no' cancels meaning and mind. Just as waiting will cancel mind, its worries, its questions; just as waiting will make you silent, so 'no' will create the same space. Different masters, different answers; but pointing to the same space.

*The monk brought this question to Enkan,
who said, "Two dead men in one coffin."*

It does not happen anywhere: two dead men in one coffin. He is saying by this statement that you are putting two dead men in one coffin: you are putting this significance, the tremendous beauty, the grace, into one coffin with Bodhidharma. But

Bodhidharma is after all a coffin just as you are, just as I am. Inside, there can be only one, not two.

Enkan's meaning is a little difficult to understand but he is saying, "Don't put contradictory things together. Mind and meaning? What has mind to do with meaning? And what has Bodhidharma to do with coming?" Even without Bodhidharma, *dhyan* was going to blossom. It is just coincidental that Bodhidharma was being used by existence to bring the message.

It reminds me of Albert Einstein. He was asked that, "If you had not discovered the theory of relativity, can you tell us how many years we would have had to wait for someone to discover it?"

Albert Einstein was certainly a very humble, sincere man. He said, "Not more than two weeks. The climate was ready. I was just a vehicle."

The people who heard this could not believe it. The theory of relativity is so difficult that the greatest philosopher of our century, Bertrand Russell, has written a book: *The ABC of Relativity*. When he was asked, "Why ABC? Why not the whole thing up to XYZ?" Bertrand Russell said, "First I have to understand that much. I only understand the ABC."

Only twelve people in the whole world were known to have had some understanding of what Albert Einstein had found. And to say that within two weeks somebody else would have discovered it shocked people. They could not believe it. They thought, "Perhaps he is joking. Perhaps he is being too humble." But it is not humbleness, it is simple truthfulness.

And the theory was found in a German philosopher's notebooks who had discovered it before Einstein. But he was a lazy man and he did not publish it. So somebody had discovered it not just after two weeks, but perhaps two months previously. But lazy men are lazy men: it remained in his papers, which he never published; they were found when he was dead. He was the real discoverer.

There is always a climate. In a certain climate, as the spring comes and thousands and thousands of flowers start blossoming, as the rain comes and clouds and clouds cover up the whole sky....

Daibai's reply, *"His coming has no meaning,"* meant, "It would have come anyway. The time was ripe." Existence can give a little rope, but not much.

The monk brought this question to Gensha, another master. *Gensha, hearing of this said, "Enkan is a clever chap."*

I would have to remind you of Enkan's answer, *"Two dead men in one coffin."*

Gensha said, *"Enkan is a clever chap."* He did not say that Enkan was enlightened – just "a clever chap." He made up the answer, which had not come from his own experience.

The same question – the meaning of Bodhidharma coming from the West – was brought to Sekitō, or "Stonehead", as he was also known.

By the way, please note: our own Sekitō has gone to Germany. He will be coming back soon. Perhaps Germany has more stoneheads than any other country. Half of my disciples are German. And it is not a coincidence that two years ago the German parliament passed an order that I cannot enter Germany. Clever chaps! They know that once I am in Germany, Germany is mine. It is better not to take the risk. For two years they have stayed on the safe side.

But it does not matter. My stoneheads go on coming here. Premda has come just today, finishing everything. Only stoneheads can do that: it needs guts. The German parliament is being very cowardly, very un-German; they should have invited me. I would have brought the dignity to Germany that it has lost because of idiots like Adolf Hitler.

Even Sardar is laughing. But let Sekitō come back and Sardar will have to face him. But he is in good form. Yesterday, he faced...not only faced, but he had to swim in from a long way away – he was outside – to meet the strange philosophical creature, sitting behind Maneesha. And they had a good dance.

Sekitō missed a great chance of meeting with another stonehead. And that stonehead has disappeared. Just one chance and one dance was enough. That is intelligence.

Sekitō said, *"Go and ask the outside post of the hall!"*

Asking such a stupid question, it is better you go to the post outside and ask. Having the opportunity of meeting an enlightened man, you should not bring such stupid questions.

Bodhidharma was just like a white cloud. Those white clouds go on traveling from one country to another country, passing boundaries without any entry visas, having no passports. They seem to be the most free people in the world. And Bodhidharma is just a white cloud; he cannot come for any special purpose; he must be just enjoying a morning walk. "But if you want to ask, go out and ask the post of the hall. Perhaps you may get the answer."

The monk said, "I don't know what you mean."

Asking a post outside the hall? I don't know what you mean.

"Nor do I," said Sekitō .

This acceptance, "Nor do I," is one of the greatest

contributions of Zen to the world. Being a not-knowing consciousness is not unworthy of respect, but is in fact the highest point of being aware, alert, conscious. It is buddhahood.

*When Suiyrō put the question to his master, Baso…*you have come across Baso again and again. He had thousands of disciples and is said to have made more people enlightened than anybody else, including Gautam Buddha. But his ways were very strange.

…Baso kicked him in the chest and knocked him down. Suiyrō was enlightened. He stood up and, clapping his hands and laughing aloud, said, "A miracle! A miracle! The hundred samadhis and the countless mysterious truths are profoundly known to me now in the tip of one hair."
He made his bows and departed.

Baso said nothing but did something. Certainly, from the outside it looks as if he kicked the chest of the inquirer. But that is a photographic description from the outside. What happened inside? Baso had not hit the other inquirers in the chest. But hitting this monk in the chest simply means: the monk was absolutely ready, he needed only a little push.

And that little push, hitting him on the chest, knocking him down, was enough. It made it clear to him why Bodhidharma had come from the West. Just to knock you down and to bring you to your center, hidden behind your chest… The enlightenment of the inquirer was so great, he laughed aloud and said, "A miracle! A miracle! That which cannot be known, I have come to experience. That which cannot be said, you have said. You have opened the doors of millions of miracles, just by a single knock."

It was almost like a ripe mango, one knock and it falls. But unripe mangoes will not fall with one knock. It is only into those who have been preparing, waiting, keeping their doors open that a man like Baso enters. Baso is very compassionate, otherwise who cares to knock anybody down, to hit them in the chest? These methods are especially Zen methods. No tradition in the world has ever known anything about these secret methods.

But things when written lose much. I would like you to experience it. Writing and reading will not help. Learn to wait till infinity. Because you are eternal, there is no hurry. Be silent and if you have found a master, if you have fallen in love with a master, then just remain bathed in his presence. Some day, the push will come.

You must have seen...birds have to push their children from the nest. It is something worth seeing because the same happens between the master and the disciple. When the egg is broken and the bird has come out of it, the mother leaves the nest, flies around the tree to give a sense, a feeling to the bird that, "You also can do it." But the poor small fellow simply flutters his wings afraid to go out into the vast unknown.

The mother goes to other trees and gives a challenge, calls the bird, "Come to me" – not in your language. The bird becomes slowly, slowly stronger and when the mother finds it is the right time, she pushes the bird out of the nest. First, the bird feels freaked out – the mother is killing him – but soon he finds that he has wings and he goes to another tree and calls back.

And once he has flown a few feet, a few miles does not matter. There are birds, for example swans, which travel three thousand miles every time, every year when the lake in the Himalayas becomes frozen. They have to come down to the plains, three thousand miles.

It is not only true about birds. One step is enough to understand that if you can step once, you can manage to travel a thousand miles. Soon the bird will be flying farther and farther away. One morning as the sun rises, the bird will be gone perhaps forever, not to return to the nest.

The master has to wait. Those days were more beautiful than the days we live in, because now if you hit somebody, you will find yourself in the police station – however much you try to say, "I am a master." However much you say, "He is my disciple and I am trying to make him awakened." It isn't going to help. You will have to appear in court.

I myself have been jailed in six jails and brought into two courts. And I could see: the people you call judges are absolutely unqualified. They don't understand even the ABC of meditation. They may know all the laws and bylaws, but they don't know themselves.

In these jails I had to spend time in – it was a strange experience – the prisoners seemed to be innocent. Perhaps out of innocence they had committed something which a clever man would have avoided. But in almost every jail, the prisoners said to me, "We are immensely happy to be in this jail at this moment, to be with you just for a night. We have only heard of people like you. But being with you, we never dreamed of it."

Only one jailer out of six jails had some sensitivity. He did not put me into the proper jail, but into the hospital. I said, "I am not sick."

He said, "You are not sick but I cannot put you

in jail. A man who is trying to free other people from jails should not be put in a jail. You rest in the hospital."

And the head nurse and nurses and the doctor were all surprised, because he used to come at least six times a day to see me. And because he was coming to see me, his assistant and his other staff members all started coming. The hospital became my ashram for three days. They all forgot that I was a prisoner. They ought not to have asked me questions related to the secrets of life, for on the third day I had to leave the jail for another jail. The government felt that his jail was destroyed, because the jailer had also allowed me a world press conference. Even his assistant said, "This is not done. It is unprecedented."

He said, "I don't care. I am on the point of retirement. At the most, they can retire me."

The government must have felt very embarrassed by the idea of having a press conference inside the jail, so immediately I was removed. But when I was coming out of the jail, the jailer said to me, "In my whole life of service I have never felt unhappy when a prisoner was released. But about you, I would love it if you were never released from this jail. In three days we have become so much accustomed to you; without you there will be an empty space. If you want to have the experience of being in jail again, please don't forget us!"

And he had tears in his eyes.

Our bodies, our minds are nothing but jails. We are imprisoned splendor. And if you go on and on, around and around, you will not find yourself and your freedom. To be is to be free. To be is to be a god. Nothing less will do to describe the fact.

Maneesha has asked:

Beloved Bhagwan,
Last night was a truly existential discourse: the beast behind me, the Buddha before me, and I danced with both!

Maneesha, the beautiful person who was behind you was not a beast. No beast is a beast. He was just wearing the coat of a beast. He was nobody else but our poor Vimal. And remember, it is not only true about Vimal. Whenever you come to real beasts, they are also wearing coats. Inside them, is the same consciousness as is in you.

The gorilla behind you was as much a buddha as the buddha before you. And in between, don't forget that you are also a buddha. Here, there is only one quality of consciousness: the consciousness of being buddhas.

But don't be cuckoos. The moment you start declaring in M.G. market that, "I am a buddha," you will be in trouble. Keep this a secret within you, unwavering, never forgetting for a single moment that buddhahood is your nature. You cannot be otherwise. Although Vimal was hiding behind a gorilla coat, still Vimal was Vimal.

The body that Vimal has is another coat, given by biology. Behind that coat, given by your society there is another layer: the mind. And within that mind is your temple, your buddha. We are searching here for nobody else but our own authentic being.

It was good of Vimal to come in a gorilla dress, because everybody is wearing different kinds of dresses. The inside has the same taste, the same sweetness, the same song, the same laughter.

Hymie Goldberg and his son, Swami Deva Herschel, are discussing Herschel's coming trip to

Poona. "You know son," says Hymie, "you can get very sick in India."

"I know," replies Herschel, "and I can get killed walking across Fifth Avenue in New York."

"Well," urges Hymie, "at least think of your mother. She is worried sick."

"She is always worried sick," snaps Herschel.

"Well," says Hymie, "this guy you are going to see, is he Jewish?"

"Hell, no," replies Herschel, "he even works on the Sabbath."

Disgusted, Hymie snaps back, "You know, son, if you carry on like this, you will amount to *nothing*."

"Wow, Dad," says Herschel, "you really *do* understand."

Swami Deva Herschel has only been in Poona for a week, when he meets a gorgeous Ma, and invites her out to dinner. They go to the Regency Hotel and feast on Italian spaghetti, Japanese sushi, and French wine.

For dessert, they choose German chocolate cake and finish up with Brazilian coffee.

When the waiter brings them the bill, Herschel finds that he has left his wallet at home. So he takes out a picture of Bhagwan Shree Rajneesh and hands it to the waiter.

"What is this?" demands the waiter.

"This," replies Herschel, "is my Zen master card!"

Granma Murphy is eighty-five years old. She tires easily, has little appetite and is sometimes confused mentally. So her son, Paddy, calls for the doctor. He arrives shortly and goes up to granma's room where he undresses her, lies her down on the bed and gives her a complete physical examination.

Half an hour later, the doctor comes downstairs.

"There is no need to worry," he explains, "there is nothing really wrong with her except her age. She will be all right."

Paddy is very relieved and goes upstairs to see her.

"Well, mother," he asks, "how did you like the doctor?"

"So, he was the *doctor,* was he?" says granma with a smile. "I thought he was a bit naughty for the priest."

Little Ernie says to his mother, "Mom, do dogs have spare parts?"

"Don't be silly," replies his mother, "how on earth could dogs have spare parts? They are alive."

"Well, then," says Ernie, "why did Dad tell Uncle Joe that when you go to visit your sister next week he is going to screw the ass off the bitch next door?"

Rupesh, beat the drum.

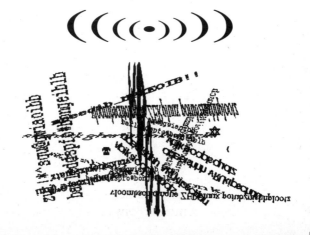

Rupesh…

Be silent, close your eyes.
Be in.
No movement.
Be as still as a stone buddha.

Rupesh, beat the drum.

Everybody falls dead.
Let the body breathe;
you be as deep within yourself as possible.
This is the quantum leap
from mind to no-mind.
This is the message for which
Bodhidharma has come from the West
to China.
The message is:
it is you;
it is in.

Rupesh, beat the drum.

Come back to life as totally as possible,
alive, fresh.

A few may still be in their graves.
For them a special beat…

That's good.
At least it will make the drums enlightened.

Okay, Maneesha?
Yes, Bhagwan.
Can we celebrate now?
YES!

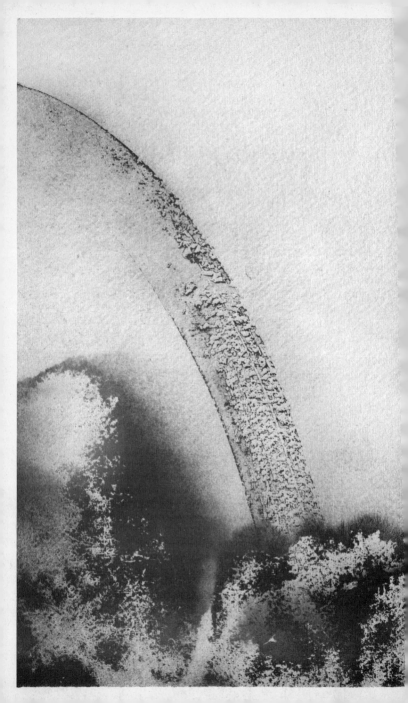

CAN A CIRCLE BE
MORE CIRCULAR?

Beloved Bhagwan,

*Baso said to his master, Nangaku,
"The way is formless. How can we see it well?"*

*Nangaku answered, "It is like the eye of the law,
possessed by the ground of mind seeing clearly
the way, the samadhi of no-form."*

Baso said, "Can it progress or decay?"

*Nangaku replied, "If it is seen as progressing
and decaying, becoming firm and dispersing,
it is not seen."*

*Another master, Enkei, was asked by a monk,
"It is said that if we see the form of things,
we see the mind. If we take a lantern as form,
what is the mind?"*

*Enkei said, "You don't understand the meaning
of the ancients."*

*The monk asked, "What is the meaning
of the ancients?"*

Enkei said, "The lantern is the mind."

*In another incident, the master, Hogen,
pointed to some bamboos, and said to a monk,
"Do you see them?"*

"I see them," replied the monk.

*"Do they come to the eye, or does the eye go to
them?" asked Hogen.*

"I have no idea at all," said the monk.

Hogen gave up and went away.

Vimal, the first thing *you* have to understand is that by becoming a dangerous, ferocious animal you gave migraine to poor Maneesha. Remember it always, falling below humanity and then sitting behind a poor girl... It is fortunate that she is still alive, you have done everything to kill her.

As a gorilla you were dancing with her: I had left the place, just because I did not want to see the dance of a gorilla. And you see the result now? Be ashamed! Give your gorilla dress to Sardar Gurudayal Singh; it does not suit you. It will suit Sardar Gurudayal Singh anywhere. He can go into the city and freak out people. He does it anyway, but in a gorilla dress, and with his laughter... Sardar Gurudayal Singh!

(His loud laughter is heard from the back of the hall.)

Take that gorilla dress from Vimal tomorrow. And as the dress reaches you, the migraine of Maneesha will disappear. It is not migraine, it is simply fear that – who knows – that gorilla may be sitting behind her again.

You have asked, Vimal:
Baso said to his master, Nangaku,
"The way is formless. How can we see it well?"
The question is very logical and rational. If the way is formless, obviously you cannot see it. To see anything it has to be objective, with a form. If it has no form, if it is infinite, how can you see it?

Baso in his own right later on proved to be one of the greatest masters, but even while he was a disciple of Nangaku, his master, his questions were immensely important. *"The way is formless."* That's what Buddha said, so there is every support for his question. And now he is asking Nangaku, *"How can we see it well?"*

But Nangaku was not in any way a smaller master. *Nangaku answered, "It is like the eye of the law, possessed by the ground of mind seeing clearly the way, the samadhi of no-form."*

The answer seems to be absolutely absurd: what he is saying makes no sense. He is saying, "There are thousands of samadhis, graves of people who have seen it and declared it as formless. I am not the only one. Its formlessness does not prevent its being seen; you just need a different vision, a different eye." In Yoga they have called it 'the third eye', which can see the infinite.

It is like the eye of the law. The word 'law' is a wrong translation of 'dharma'. It is always difficult changing great things from one language to another. The Sanskrit 'dharma', the Pali 'dhamma' can mean religion and can also mean the law, because religion is nothing but the law of existence, the very order of this universe.

Nangaku answered, "It is like the eye of the law, possessed by the ground of mind. Underneath your mind there are roots of your being, which possess your ultimate vision, the third eye. *…seeing clearly the way, the samadhi of no-form."*

This whole existence has no limitations, nowhere is the boundary. Now physicists are in difficulty… These small questions and these small anecdotes have become tremendously significant for modern physicists, because they also are questioning if the universe has limits; and then you have to accept something which you have not seen! Nobody has seen the boundary where the universe ends: it is purely a hypothesis.

Up to now science has been trying to believe that somewhere far away, millions and trillions of light-years away, there must be a boundary. They say that everything has a boundary: we may not be able to see it, but it has to be there. But that is only an assumption. With Albert Einstein's researches the assumption has fallen down. One of the greatest achievements of Albert Einstein was to make the universe free from boundaries. His work is as important as the work of all the mystics of the world.

The mystics have been trying to make your consciousness boundary-less. Albert Einstein tried to make this whole universe unbounded, unlimited, infinite, although there is no way to prove it. But nor can the contrary be proved either. In the absence of contrary proof it seems to be rational to accept, at least as a hypothesis, that existence has no boundary. It cannot have, because to make a boundary you will need another existence. Who will make the boundary? What will be beyond the boundary? And if there is still something beyond the boundary, it is still the universe. It can be seen very simply that boundaries don't belong to existence.

But mystics are not concerned with the objective world. Their concern is with the inner world, the inner universe of consciousness. Has it a form? And if there is no form, how can you see when somebody is self-realized? How can you see that you have seen yourself? Only form can be seen.

Nangaku changes the whole situation. He says, "It is not a question of your ordinary eyes. Of course they can only see the form, but deep in your very being is a capacity to know the formless".

But Baso was no ordinary disciple.

Baso said, "Can it progress or decay? I accept your hypothesis, but I have a few questions." Baso says, "Can it progress, the no-form, the unlimited consciousness, can it progress or decay?"

He is putting his master to a fire test.

*Nangaku replied, "If it is seen as progressing
and decaying, becoming firm and dispersing,
it is not seen."*

To ask whether perfection can be more perfect is
absurd. Perfection is perfection: it cannot be more,
it cannot be less. Take a small example: can a circle
be more circular, or less circular? A circle is a circle;
it can be neither more circular, nor less circular.

"Your very question shows," Nangaku said to
Baso, "that you have not seen it. Your third eye is
still fast asleep. Your mind is young, your intelligence is great, but your inner eye has not yet
opened; it is a bud, it has not become a rose."

*Another master, Enkei, was asked by a monk,
"It is said that if we see the form of things,
we see the mind. If we take a lantern as form,
what is the mind?"*

*Enkei said, "You don't understand the meaning
of the ancients."*

*The monk asked, "What is the meaning
of the ancients?"*

Enkei said, "The lantern is the mind."

This is something to be understood. When you
bring something before a mirror, it reflects it so perfectly that you can say that the mirror has become
it. If the mind can see…it is a mirror. Your eyes are
mirrors and nothing else. They reflect. And in reflecting they become things, whatever they reflect.

Looking into a person's eyes, you can discover
his whole personality, his whole psychology, his
whole mind and the mask. The eyes reflect not
only the outside world, they also reflect your inner
world: how deep you are, whether you are just a
surface, a thin layer of water that reflects, or an
ocean.

When Baso became the master himself, succeeding his own master Nangaku, before initiating any disciple he used to look into their eyes. He would bring the disciple closer and look into his eyes. And Baso looking into your eyes is almost as if you are in the hands of a lion. Just by his look...the penetration of his vision was as sharp as a razor blade. He had made a few people enlightened just by looking into their eyes. Their minds disappear: they cannot confront the eyes of the master, Baso. Baso is a very rare master.

The monk asked, "What is the meaning
of the ancients?"
Enkei said, "The lantern is the mind."

When you are seeing the lantern, if you are not wavering within, in a very miraculous way, the reflection and the reflected become one, the observed and the observer become one, the loved and the lover become one.

In such small statements so much is hidden that on each statement a great philosophy can be based.

In another incident, the master, Hogen,
pointed to some bamboos, and said to a monk,
"Do you see them?"

"I see them," replied the monk, not understanding that when a master asks you, "Do you see it?" he does not mean your ordinary eyes. A master's finger is always pointing to the inner, not to the outer. But the poor monk thought that the master is asking whether he can see the bamboos.

"Yes, I see them," replied the monk.
"Do they come to the eye, or does the eye go to them?"

How do you manage to see? Somebody has to go: either your eyes go to the bamboos, or the bamboos come to your eyes. Which way does it happen?

"I have no idea at all," said the monk, feeling utterly defeated, not knowing what to say, because the fact is, no one goes, no one comes. The eyes are in their place and the bamboos are in their place. There is no going and there is no coming. Do you think when the full moon is reflected in the silent lake, the lake goes to the moon, or the moon comes to the lake? The moon remains in its place, the lake remains in its place, but the lake's silence, its mirrorlike surface reflects.

The poor monk could not say that: "Nobody goes, nobody comes, everything is in its own place, there is no coming, there is no going."

Because he could not answer, *Hogen gave up and went away.*

Hogen was a very strict master, not as compassionate as Baso or Gautam Buddha. He had the same experience, but he was very stern with his disciples, always wanting them to answer rightly. You could not deceive Hogen, nor could you ask for any compassion from him.

He used to say, "All compassion is dangerous," because what is the inner implication of compassion? It means allowing ignorance. He would not allow any ignorance: he would chop your head if it was needed, but compassion was not his method.

Rather than explaining to the disciple, he simply left and went away, without saying a word. This is his way of saying, "You are not worthy of me, you are not worthy of Zen. You cannot answer a simple thing, that in a reflection nothing goes, nothing comes, everything remains in its place." And in existence the case is the same: no going, no coming – just be.

You can feel here, nothing is going, nothing is coming, a tremendous silence. The bamboos are not even making their commentary.

Poor Maneesha is not here, but her question is. She has asked,

Beloved Bhagwan,
Thank You – thank existence – thank You – that
You don't give up as easily as Hogen.

But Maneesha, where are *you?* The master is here and the disciple has given up! And this whole mess is being created by Vimal who is sitting in front of me.

Although you are not here, your question is significant for everyone. I am not Hogen. I will haunt you even in your graves! I will see you, however far you escape. I am haunting already all over the world and I am still alive. Once I am dead, then this world cannot prevent me; no law, no parliament, no country can make barriers for me; then I will be all over the place, tickling people to wake up. Even now I am not doing anything nasty to anybody, just tickling.

And I want you to remember that there are always a few stupid people, who come here out of curiosity. If you find any stupid person around you, not doing the gibberish, tickle! Do it from all sides; it is a religious duty. Don't leave the poor fellow alone. He should not go home the same as he came here. He should go laughing, forgetting all his misery and business. So while you are doing your gibberish, just take care that nobody is sitting silent. When you are silent, then take care that nobody is moving.

This is not an ordinary assembly, a crowd, this is a place where everybody has to become enlightened, in spite of himself!

I am a different kind of man, Maneesha.

Before you start your gibberish…from today I will not move my hands, I will watch you. And if I see somebody sitting silently, I am going to point. Then whoever he is, just tickle him. I have tickled you enough. Now it is your dharma!

Before our meditation begins I have to prepare the ground for you.

Swami Deva Coconut has a terrible pain in his back. When it becomes unbearable, he reluctantly goes to Ruby Hall clinic to visit Doctor Ekdam Kwality, the specialist, to have him diagnose his problem.

Doctor Ekdam Kwality examines Coconut carefully, takes an X-ray and asks him to come back the next day.

When Coconut returns, Ekdam Kwality says, "Well, I have studied the X-ray carefully, and your problem can be cured by an operation, followed by two weeks in the hospital, and then six months lying on your back – at an approximate cost of twenty-five thousand rupees!"

"Jesus Christ," cries Coconut, "I can't afford all that!"

"Okay," says Ekdam Kwality. "Then for twenty-five rupees I can retouch the X-ray!"

After ten years of marriage, Boris and Betty Bunkovitz get divorced. Betty wins custody of their young son, Bert, and three hundred dollars a month in child support from Boris.

On the first of every month, Betty sends Bert to Boris to pick up the money. And every month the check is waiting.

On his eighteenth birthday, Bert goes once again to Boris. But this time, as Boris hands Bert the check, Boris says, "Bert, when you give this check to your mother, tell her it is the last check I am going to send her…and watch the expression on her face!"

Returning home, Bert says to Betty,

"Mum, Boris told me to watch the expression on your face when I tell you that this is your last check."

"Is that so?" says Betty. "Then, I want you to go straight back over there and watch the expression on Boris' face, when you tell him that he is not your father!"

Sardar Gurudayal Singh from Poona decides to go to Singapore for some shopping. He goes into a shop, dressed in his best flowing robes, curly shoes and turban, and asks, "What is the price of that video machine in the window?"

The salesman answers, "Sorry, sir, we don't sell to Indians."

To Sardar Gurudayal Singh this is very shocking. He goes back to his hotel and dresses as an Englishman in a pin-striped suit, with all his hair pushed up into a bowler hat. Back at the shop he asks, "My good man, what is the price of that video in the window?"

To his dismay the seller replies, "Sorry, sir, we don't sell to Indians!"

So this time Sardar Gurudayal Singh dresses as an American. He lets all his hair down, puts on Bermuda shorts, T-shirt and sunglasses, and goes back into the shop. "Hey, man!" he says. "How much for that far-out video machine?" But he gets the same reply. In exasperation Sardar Gurudayal Singh cries, "How do you know that I am an Indian?"

"That is easy," replies the seller. "The article in the window that you desire is not a video, it is a washing machine!"

Rupesh, give the first beat and everybody goes into gibberish.

(Bhagwan watches very carefully, looking slowly from far left to far right, his finger ready to point to anybody who is not doing the gibberish properly!)

Rupesh…

Be silent,
the way the bamboos are silent.
Just be,
close your eyes and be within.

No movement,
either of the mind or of the body…
Just be!
Now and here,
a pure isness.

Deeper and deeper…
Don't spare anything.
You have nothing to lose
by going deeper into yourself,
but everything to gain.

At the very center of your being
is the door of the kingdom of God.
You don't even have to open it;
it is open, it is waiting.

Come in. You are always welcome,
come in!

Rupesh, give the beat…

Everybody falls dead.
Let your body breathe;
relax totally
so that you can move even deeper
into your being.
Have the taste of this tremendous silence,
feel the beatitude of this moment.
This is what I have called the quantum leap,
from mind to no-mind.

Rupesh, call the dead back to life, give the drum a good beat...

One more...

Come back, fresh and alive,
coming from the innermost sources
of your life
and consciousness.

Fresh and fragrant,
fearless and free,
just pure individuals
as existence always wanted you to be.

Okay, Vimal?
Yes, Bhagwan.
Can we celebrate?
YES!

GORILLA, SIR,
BE A GENTLEMAN

Beloved Bhagwan,

*On the occasion of his first visiting Rinzai,
Kankei had hardly crossed the threshold,
when Rinzai suddenly seized him by the lapels.*

Kankei said, "I understand! I understand!"

*Rinzai let go of him, and said,
"For the time being I'll omit the twenty blows!"*

*Kankei lived with Rinzai from that time on,
and afterwards used to say, "When I saw
Rinzai, there was no talking or explanation.
Now I am quite full, and feel no hunger."*

*Bashō told how he first met with the master,
Nanto.*

*He said, "When I was twenty-eight years old,
I went on a pilgrimage, and reached where
Nanto was living. Ascending the rostrum, Nanto
said, 'All you people, if you are enlightened,
you will come out of your mother's womb and
roar like a lion. You know what this roaring
means?'"*

*Bashō added, "Immediately my mind and body
were rendered motionless, and I stopped with
him for five years."*

Maneesha, before I discuss the anecdote I have to say something about your migraine. As I said yesterday, the moment the beast disappears Maneesha's migraine will disappear too. I am not a prophet, but Vimal did make a very existential statement, a real, alive, existential anecdote.

His being covered in a gorilla coat should not be understood as an individual expression. Everybody is covered with something that is animal. Man has not yet been born! Bodies have changed, but it is your mind that is still struggling in deep forests. You have to be freed from your gorilla coats.

In this century an unprecedented one hundred million people have been killed in wars. You call this a sane humanity? And rather than helping sanity, people go on insisting that man should not discover himself.

Just a few days ago Turiya was in the West and she participated in a new kind of therapy, Fischer-Hoffman, which is doing immense harm. Ordinarily I don't speak against stupidities. But this stupid effort of Fischer-Hoffman therapy has to be demolished completely from its very roots.

Their effort is to make your ego stronger, although they don't say that is what they are doing; they say they are making your individuality independent.

They don't even know the difference between individuality and personality. In the name of individuality they are destroying all possibilities of your spiritual growth. You will be left alone with your ego.

They are teaching people…and they are the most expensive therapists now; their training course runs for one year, and they earn millions of dollars by making people free from their mothers, from their fathers, from their wives, from their husbands, from their masters.

Before they do any more harm, I appoint Turiya to start here an Anti-Fischer-Hoffman Therapy group to make it clear that to have your ego does not mean you are free; it simply means you are encaged in your own mind.

Before you can be really independent you have to know who you are, who it is beating in your heart; you have to know the universal element, the existential part of your being. Without knowing it, you will be falling again and again into different kinds of bondages. You may be freed from one church, another church will open its door and welcome you. You will be freed from mothers and fathers, then Fischer-Hoffman will become your father and mother.

Unless you know that you are alone and enough unto yourself, not borrowed knowledge, but your own *experience*... The whole effort here is to bring you to a point where freedom blossoms. I am not a fetter to you. Love can never be a fetter, it can never be a prison, and if it is a prison, then it is not love. I know myself; I am sharing with you my delight, my celebration, my arriving home. You are absolutely independent; I am not asking anything from you, just trying to take away that which you are not and consistently forcing on you that which you are.

The whole of Western history is ego-centered. They have known nothing about enlightenment. And without enlightenment there is no freedom, no truth, no fearlessness, no dance and no celebration of being. All the therapists here have to help Turiya to create Anti-Fischer-Hoffmann Therapy. And I invite the people who are running the therapy in the West to come here and face me. Ego is not freedom.

Ego is your worst enemy: it is not your strength, it is just a mock-up; it is not you, not even your photograph, not even your shadow.

I want you to know who is in the innermost being of your interiority. Only that can bring freedom to you. The ego is the last thing to disappear before man can arrive on the earth; otherwise everybody is a gorilla. It does not matter whether you have a gorilla coat or not.

And it was good of Vimal to appear in a gorilla coat, of course unconsciously, not knowing the implications; but he created a migraine in Maneesha. That is very symbolic. Man has been the gorilla all along, creating thousands of migraines in women, all kinds of slaveries and exploitations, preventing their spiritual growth.

This place is devoted to absolute freedom, but freedom does not mean license, it means tremendous responsibility. To be is to be responsible: only animals can have licentiousness. To be a man, to have the dignity of being a man means you have accepted the responsibility. You will not blame anything on anyone. Now you always look within for whatever happens to you.

A survey in Brazil of the primitive people, who have been killed or moved into deep forests around the Amazon, has shown – and this survey was done by professional psychoanalysts – that their methods of curing people's madness are more effective than our so-called psychology. Their methods are very simple, but are based on something totally different. Their basis is, unless a man's spirituality is cured, his psychology is going to remain sick. Once your being is cured then mind itself is understood as sickness. You don't need it. What you need is a clarity which mind is preventing.

A man can only be a man if he has attained to the state of no-mind, if he has taken the quantum leap we are talking about. It is from animal to man, from mind to no-mind.

Just today I received information from my sannyasin representative in America that he was interviewed by the press, because they have become worried that I am going to enter the presidential election in America? And there is no law that can prevent me, although everybody knows it is a joke. I cannot fall that low. Twenty percent of American presidents have been murdered, so that is the most stupid place to be. A twenty percent chance of being murdered…! Even men like Abraham Lincoln and Kennedy are no exceptions. The best America has produced it has destroyed.

Just as a joke I have said, "Yes," to the Global Promoters, the biggest promoting agency in America, to make it known to everybody in America that I am still alive and kicking. Who cares about being the president of America, I am not that stupid.

The press has also asked the Immigration Department, "What do you say, now that Bhagwan is going to enter the presidential election?"

And the chief of the Immigration Department said, "This is possible only if God wants it."

It is good to know that the Immigration Department of America will at least not prevent God from coming into America. And also it seems that the American Immigration Department – which fought me for five years and had not the guts even to arrest me – seems to be a very faithful, religious, God-loving company. These are the people who have killed God also, because anybody who is preparing to destroy this planet – and America is number one…

It is so hilarious that on the one hand they go on saying they believe that God created the world, and now Ronald Reagan is going to destroy it. Is this what fundamentalist Christianity means? In a way it is very symbolic. God is killed by the priests, God is killed by the believers. God is known only by the meditators, not as a separate entity hiding somewhere millions of light-years away, but someone breathing within your heart. Only a meditator becomes a temple of God, only a meditator becomes an answer to all kinds of atheistic suspicions.

I was amazed also to receive today another piece of research, done by American psychoanalysts in China. Up to now psychoanalysts have believed that possessiveness is biological, it is instinctive. But they were surprised to discover that Chinese children are not as possessive as American children. Chinese children share more than American children, are less aggressive than American children. They had to change their whole idea and for the first time accept that possessiveness and aggression are not biological but cultural, educational, social.

That's what I have been telling you, that whatever is wrong in you has not come from nature, but is part of your social and cultural heritage. Unless you become totally free from culture, so-called civilization, and show the strength of being alone, man will never arrive on this planet.

Vimal's existential statement is worth appreciating. He did it well, without knowing that he was exposing everybody else too. You all have to look deep down and drop your gorilla coats. Find out the diamond of your being, inside.

Gautam Buddha even had a series of lectures, called the Diamond Sutra, to discover the diamond within you. Nobody can give it to you, you already have it; only, you have to be shaken awake.

On the occasion of his first visiting Rinzai,
Kankei had hardly crossed the threshold, when
Rinzai suddenly seized him by the lapels.
Kankei said, "I understand! I understand!"
Rinzai let go of him, and said, "For the time
being I will omit the twenty blows!"

Rinzai was one of the loveliest masters in the history of Zen. He brought Zen from China to Japan, but he had lived with Chinese masters. He carried the same flame Bodhidharma took from India to China. He had something of the same greatness, beauty, and the absurd approach to awaken you. Anything rational your mind absorbs, and goes on sleeping: something absurd which the mind cannot make any sense of is absolutely needed to cut the mind in a single blow.

On the occasion of his first visiting Rinzai,
Kankei had hardly crossed the threshold, when
Rinzai suddenly seized him by the lapels.
Kankei immediately *said, "I understand! I*
understand!"

He knew that this man had been beating people to wake them up. He had been known to throw people from windows out of his room, jump upon them and ask them, "Do you understand?"

Nothing was impossible for this man. Out of fear, *Kankei said, "I understand! I understand!* Just don't start…this is enough!"

Rinzai let go of him, and said, "For the time being I will omit the twenty blows!" You require to be beaten at least twenty times. But for the time being I will leave it, you are not ripe enough. You are so fearful that I have not said anything and you start shouting, 'I understand!'. You have not even crossed the threshold. You are not worthy to have a taste of my stick. *"For the time being, I will omit the twenty blows."* Be ripe, be yourself, be worthy of a master's reward. And the master can reward you in only one way: by waking you up. Whatsoever means he has to adopt are arbitrary.

Kankei lived with Rinzai from that time on,
and afterwards used to say, "When I saw

Rinzai, there was no talking or explanation.
Now I am quite full, and feel no hunger."

Six years he lived with Rinzai. Not a single word passed from Rinzai's lips towards Kankei. Silence was the only communication. But in six years' time, Kankei was able to say, *"When I saw Rinzai, there was no talking or explanation. Now I am quite full, and feel no hunger."*

A master, just by his presence, can also awaken you. It all depends on you. If your longing to be awake in this sleeping world is total, then this very moment you will find yourself full, without any hunger.

Bashō told how he first met with the master, Nanto.

He said, "When I was twenty-eight years old, I went on a pilgrimage, and reached where Nanto was living. Ascending the rostrum, Nanto said, 'All you people, if you are enlightened, you will come out of your mother's womb and roar like a lion. You know what this roaring means?'"

Bashō added, "Immediately my mind and body were rendered motionless, and I stopped with him for five years."

Just the way he said 'roaring', just the way he was, his presence, his heartbeat; and Bashō lived with him for five years without a single word passing between the master and the disciple.

And Bashō became one of the greatest masters in his own right. He deserved it. Every man of silence, of love, of no-mind is a born master. Whether he has disciples or not does not matter. The master can be alone and yet be the master. His being a master does not depend on followers, on disciples, but on his own awareness.

Turiya, this has to be the basic philosophy for the Anti-Hoff-Fischerman. I call it Hoff-Fischerman because to say Hoffman is not right. Man cannot be 'half', even in Germany. Either man is total, full or he is absent.

You have to work out, Turiya, in detail the process by which the ego is destroyed without destroying the individuality. Individuality has to be sharpened, freedom has to be made more and more fragrant. Everybody has to be given wings and the whole sky as their territory, unlimited.

Maneesha has asked a question:

Beloved Bhagwan,
Oh dear! A lion now! He slipped in after another sutra had already been selected and insisted on being included, saying you would understand. Sorry, but what to do. I am afraid the word has spread.

Don't be worried,

Sutra or no sutra, I am here to hit you awake. This sutra or another sutra…these are just arbitrary means. I will use every possible means to destroy your unconsciousness and sleep. I want thousands of flames around me, dancing in a festival of lights.

Before you start your meditation, a few cold drinks will be good.

Old man Finkelstein manages to get a date with his secretary, Miss Willing, but is worried about his aging equipment. So he goes to see Dr. Bones and asks for something to restore his youthful vigor. Bones gives him two pills and says, "Take these with your dinner tonight and you will be able to perform like a bull."

So Fink and Miss Willing go to the best restaurant in town and when they have ordered their soup, Fink calls the waiter and says, "Put these pills into my soup before you serve it."

The waiter disappears. They wait for half an hour and still the soup has not been served, so Fink angrily calls the waiter and says, "What the hell has happened to our soup?"

"I am sorry, sir," replies the waiter, "but I put the pills into your soup and now I am waiting for the noodles to lie down again."

Every time Tex rides his horse through the Indian village, he waves cheerfully at the old chief. In reply, the old chief holds up his hand with his middle finger pointing upwards. Then he turns his hands so that his finger points horizontally.

Tex gets curious to know what the old chief is trying to communicate to him. So, one day, he gets off his horse in the Indian village and goes to the chief's tent. "I know what it means," says Tex, "when you wave at me with the finger straight up. But what does it mean when you turn your finger sideways?"

"It means," says the old chief, "that I don't like your horse, either!"

Father O'Leary goes to a farm in order to buy a horse. He sees a beautiful one that he likes and asks if he can try it.

"Sure," says the farmer, "but I have to tell you something. That horse used to belong to the bishop, and if you want the horse to move, you have to say, 'My God!' and if you want him to stop, you have to say, 'Hallelujah'."

"That's okay," says the priest and jumps up on

the horse and says, "My God!" The horse promptly moves off and Father O'Leary is seen galloping into the mountains.

The priest is shouting, "My God! My God!" and the horse is really moving. But suddenly, Father O'Leary sees that they are coming to the edge of a cliff and in panic he yells, "Stop! Stop!" but the horse keeps on going. Then he remembers and shouts, "Hallelujah!"

The horse stops, right on the edge of the cliff, and, looking down, Father O'Leary says, "My God!"

Rupesh…
I am going to watch that nobody remains silent. You are so full of gibberish. Throw it out! First clean the ground, then silence descends on its own.

Rupesh, give the first beat.

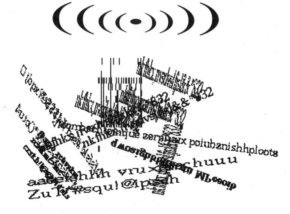

Rupesh…

Be silent. Gather yourself inwards.
Close your eyes.
No movement. Just be.
Beautiful is the moment
and blessed you are.

Rupesh…

Fall dead. Let the body breathe but you go on,
in and in.
This is the door from animal to man,
from mind to no-mind,
the quantum leap.
Fearlessly enter into your interiority.
This is you.
Feel it, rejoice in it.
This moment contains eternity.

Rupesh…

Bring everybody back to life.

One more beat.

Come back to life, alive, fresh,
soaked in your own consciousness,
cleansed by no-mind,
having touched eternity and tasted immortality
which is your basic right, your birthright.

Okay, Maneesha?
Yes, Bhagwan.
Can we celebrate now?
YES!

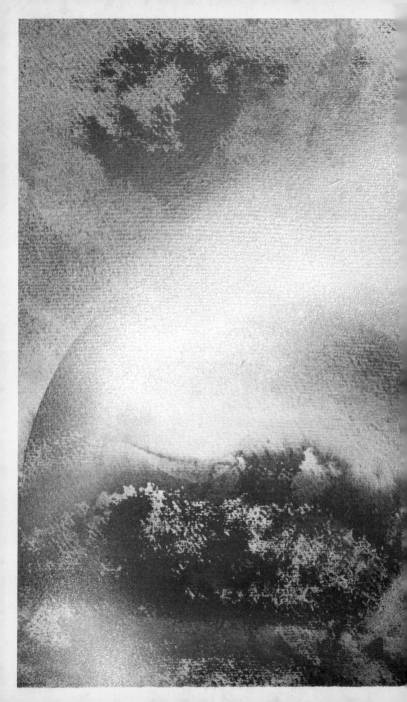

ONE CANNOT
HAVE A PROBLEM

Beloved Bhagwan,

*After a lecture to the monks one morning,
Yakusan was approached by a monk, who said,
"I have a problem. Will you solve it for me?"*

*"I will solve it at the next lecture,"
Yakusan answered.*

*That evening, when all the monks had gathered
in the hall, Yakusan called out loudly,
"The monk who told me this morning he had
a problem, come up here immediately!"*

*As soon as the monk stepped forward to stand
in front of the audience, the master left his seat
and roughly took hold of the monk.
"Look!" he said. "This fellow has a problem!"*

*He then pushed the monk aside and returned to
his room without giving the evening lecture.*

*When Kyōzan was living at Kannon Temple,
he put up a notice-board on which it said,
"No questions while sutras are being read!"*

*A monk came to visit the master, and just at
that time Kyōzan was reading the sutra,
so the monk stood beside him until Kyōzan
had finished reading and rolled up the sutra.
Kyōzan said, "Do you understand?"*

*The monk replied, "I was not reading the sutra
– how could I understand it?"*

Kyōzan said, "You will understand later."

*The monk afterwards brought the matter up to
Gontō, who said, "That old roshi! What I think
is that, properly speaking, those old scraps of
paper that were buried are still with us."*

Zen is not in the anecdotes. It is just like a fragrance around a roseflower: you cannot catch hold of it, but you can smell it. Zen needs sensitivity – not intellectual, not of the mind, but of your total being.

These anecdotes from different angles point to the same thing.

After a lecture to the monks one morning, Yakusan was approached by a monk, who said, "I have a problem. Will you solve it for me?"

In the first place, nobody can solve anybody else's problem. Deep down you don't have a problem at all, because you are the answer. How can you have a problem? The mind is full of problems, but the mind is not your reality.

Yakusan must have been a very compassionate master. He said, *"I will solve it at the next lecture."*

He is giving time to the monk to see the point. The next lecture means tomorrow, so it means that which never comes. "Drop the problem here! Don't wait for the answer to come from outside sometime in the future."

But Yakusan is known to be very kind. He said, *"I will solve it at the next lecture."*

That evening, when all the monks had gathered in the hall, Yakusan called out loudly, "The monk who told me this morning he had a problem, come up here immediately!"

As soon as the monk stepped forward to stand in front of the audience, the master left his seat and roughly took hold of the monk.

"Look!" he said. "This fellow has a problem!"

He then pushed the monk aside and returned to his room without giving the evening lecture.

He has answered in that immediacy, when he called the monk to come before the audience.

*As soon as the monk stepped forward to stand
in front of the audience, the master left his seat
and roughly took hold of the monk.*
"Look, this fellow has a problem!"

This is a very strange thing, because one cannot
have a problem! One simply *is*. All problems are
imposed by others on you: you are born as innocence. Innocence has immense clarity to see the
wonder that surrounds you, but it has no problems.
The questioning will be taught at a later stage,
because without questions the mind cannot exist.
Mind is nothing but another name for questioning.

You can try a small thing as an experiment. If
you go backwards in time, you will stop somewhere near the age of three or four. Beyond that
your memory has not recorded anything. It simply
means the first three or four years you lived in
tremendous innocence, surrounded by the beauty
of the world, of the people, of the trees, of the
ocean; not asking why, but simply being together
with whatever surrounds you, enjoying, rejoicing,
dancing. Mind has not come in yet.

Our whole educational system is programmed to
create the mind in you and to destroy the wonder,
to destroy the poetry of your life and to force you
to understand the prose and the prosaic.

Yakusan was right when he told the audience,
"Look, this fellow has a problem!" Not even the
bamboos have problems. This is a strange fellow!
And standing before a silent audience of disciples,
the poor monk must have forgotten at least for a
split second his mind and his problem.

This was the strategy of Yakusan; he has given
the answer without uttering even a single word.
Without even asking, "What is the problem?" he has
answered it. And because he has answered a great

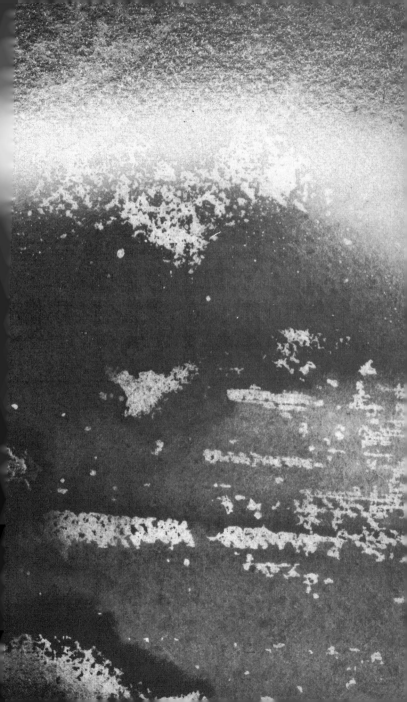

problem, *he then pushed the monk aside*. By his gesture he is saying, "Push the mind aside!" *And returned to his room without giving the evening lecture*. Returning to his room simply means returning to his inner being, indicating to everybody, "Return to your inner being."

Now, there is nothing else to be said. In a small anecdote so much is throbbing, and with so much intensity. If you can be immediate, you can get the taste of your own being. You can feel this silence.

When Kyōzan was living at Kannon,
he put up a notice-board on which it said,
"No questions while sutras are being read!"

The sutras are Buddhist scriptures.

A monk came to visit the master, and just at
that time Kyōzan was reading the sutra,
so the monk stood beside him until Kyōzan
had finished reading and rolled up the sutra.
Kyōzan said, "Do you understand?"
The monk replied, "I was not reading the sutra –
how could I understand it?"

The monk missed the great opportunity of understanding. The truth is not written in the sutra, but in closing the sutra, in dropping all the past, howsoever beautiful.

When he closed the sutra, he was indicating that when you are finished with all sutras, understanding arises on its own. It does not come out of any book, any scripture, any sutra. That's why he asked a very absurd question, *"Do you understand?"*

The poor monk was just waiting to ask something, waiting for when the reading of the sutra was finished and he could ask the question. But the master is always ahead of the disciple; before he could utter even a single word, *Kyōzan said, "Do you understand?"*

*The monk replied, "I was not reading
the sutra – how could I understand it?"*

The monk is showing his mediocre mind, showing
that he does not understand the language of those
who know, is showing his ignorance without even
being aware that if Kyōzan asks, *"Do you understand?"* he perfectly knows that he was reading the
sutra, rather than the monk. But when in the close
proximity of a disciple the master closes the sutra,
he is saying something without saying it. He is saying, "The moment you are free of sutras, you are
free of mind and all your problems will disappear.
Please don't ask them!"

Kyōzan said, "You will understand later."

This moment you missed; I had given you a great
opportunity of my presence and my silence, I did
everything to show you that the sutra has to be finished. Unfortunately you missed, but don't be worried, you will understand later.

*The monk afterwards brought the matter up to
Gontō, who said, "That old roshi!"* 'Roshi' means
the master, the old master. *"What I think is that,
properly speaking, those old scraps of paper that
were buried are still with us."*

Now he is taking the monk to the same space
which he missed when Kyōzan closed the sutra. He
is saying that, "We are still filled with *old scraps of
paper that were buried:* they are still within us.
That's why you missed that opportunity, a great
opportunity. Otherwise you would have found the
answer: you are the answer!"

Maneesha has asked:

*Beloved Bhagwan,
That poor monk was not lucky enough to be here
in Buddha Hall, because my experience is that*

problems seldom show their face when you are around. They just scuttle away, feeling very petty and out of place, and only slowly re-emerge hours later.

Maneesha, you are right, because everyone who is here is here out of an intense longing to know, to feel, to be. With me, the moment your heartbeat synchronizes, your problems start disappearing. But you have to be aware, because they don't go far away; they just wait outside Buddha Hall. This is the tragedy: when you are going out of Buddha Hall, they jump up again.

I am reminded of a man who had gone to Ramakrishna, asking for his blessings, because he was going to Kashi, the holy place for the Hindus, to have a dip in the holy Ganges – although the same Ganges was flowing by the side of Ramakrishna's hut. The man said, "Bless me, I am going to Kashi to take a holy dip."

Ramakrishna was a very simple man, a villager, but a man of great insight. He said to the man, "I have no objection: I can bless you, but I have to remind you about one thing. Have you seen that by the side of the Ganges there are tall trees?"

He said, "Yes."

Ramakrishna said, "When you take the dip in the Ganges, it is true, all your sins will jump out of your head; but they are not finished. How long can you remain immersed in the water of the Ganges? Sometime you will have to come out."

The man said, "Sometime? Even a few seconds are enough. But why are you saying that?"

Ramakrishna said, "Remember those tall trees. All the sins are sitting there, waiting for you to come out. Then they jump on you, and my experience is that sometimes even other people's sins which are left sitting…because once in a while a person takes a dip and dies. Now where do his sins go? They will wait on the trees for some other idiot and will immediately jump on you. So rather than depending on the Ganges, just take a dip here. And remember, by taking a dip you cannot get rid of your sins."

The word 'sin' is very significant. Christianity has corrupted it. In origin it means 'forgetfulness'. According to me, except for forgetfulness there is no sin: and except for awareness there is no virtue. And if you are aware, there are no sins and no problems; nothing has to be solved, everything is exactly as it should be.

Can't you feel this holy Ganges of silence you are all drowned in? But when you get out of Buddha Hall, be very careful. Don't let your old mind and your old self take possession of you. It is waiting there, just by the side of the bamboos.

I have placed bamboos around Buddha Hall, so that your problems, your sins can have a resting place. Avoid! Let them rest there, they cannot do any harm to the bamboos – particularly to bamboos, because bamboos are so hollow; they will get lost in the hollowness of the bamboos. Meanwhile you escape to your inner room.

The bamboos are asking for a few laughs. Even the clouds are not silent. A few laughs before we enter into our daily meditation.

A New Age musician from California is convinced that wild animals have a friendly, loving nature, which will respond to beautiful music.

To test his theory, he goes to the African jungle, finds a clearing in the forest, and starts to softly play his guitar. Within minutes, from out of the jungle, animals of all shapes and sizes begin to appear. Monkeys, snakes, giraffes, zebras, lions, and hippos, all are sitting together in the clearing, enchanted by the soft music.

Suddenly, there is a banging and crashing in the bushes and an old crocodile comes lumbering out of the forest. He stops, looks at the guy, opens his huge jaws, and – snap – swallows the poor musician in one bite. The other animals are furious.

"Look here, you idiot," roars the lion. "We were enjoying that!"

The crocodile looks at him blankly, puts a hand to his ear and says, "What?!"

At the Russian Intercontinental Nuclear Missile Control Center, a drunken soldier is dusting the missile control panel.

Suddenly an enraged Russian general comes puffing and panting into the room.

"What are you doing, you son-of-a-bitch?" he shouts.

"I am dusting the control panel," hiccups the soldier drunkenly.

"Okay," snaps the general, "then where the hell has England gone?"

Henri, the gallant Frenchman, has a new girl-friend called Sylvie, and he is crazy about her.

One afternoon Sylvie is waiting for him in bed in her Paris apartment, when Henri comes in. He is overcome by passion, takes off his hat and throws it out of the open window. Then he takes off his new coat and throws that out too. Sylvie shrieks with delight. Then Henri takes off his shoes and throws them out too.

"Henri, cheri," cries Sylvie, "what are you doing? Don't throw away your beautiful new clothes!"

"Do not worry, my darling," replies Henri. "By the time I am finished they will all have gone out of fashion!"

After he has left the White House, Ronald Reagan is still hankering for public office, so he decides to run for sheriff in a small rural community in California.

He sets out to visit all the farms in the neighborhood, and carries a notebook to mark down the results of each visit.

At one farmhouse, as he gets out of his car, he is met by Grandma Gittelman, holding a broom.

Grandma takes one look to see who it is and starts shouting, "Get out of here, you bum!"

"Wait," says Reagan, "I just came to ask if you would vote for me as county sheriff."

"Vote for *you?*" scoffs grandma. "You are not fit to walk the streets. You should be locked up! Now get lost."

Ronald Reagan gets back in his car and drives off fast down the road. When he gets a safe distance away he takes out his notebook and looks up Grandma Gittelman's name. Opposite it he writes: "doubtful."

Now, the first step of throwing out all your rubbish, gibberish, insanity. Rupesh, give the beat and everybody goes crazy...

Rupesh…

Be silent,
close your eyes, no movement,
just go in.
This is the holy temple of your being.

Rupesh, give the beat…

Everybody dies.
Die totally to the past, so you can be reborn.
Resurrection is possible
only if you die to the past.
You can live every moment totally new.
There is no other life than *now!*

This is the quantum leap
from mind to no-mind.
Go deeper, deeper, deeper.
Don't be afraid,
it is your own being, your own sky!

Rupesh, give the beat, bring everyone back to life…

Come back,
fresh, alive, radiant, centered,
a joy unto yourself, a peace that passeth
understanding.
This is your splendor, your glory,
this is your prayer and your gratitude
to existence.

Okay, Maneesha?
Yes, Bhagwan.
Can we celebrate now?
YES!

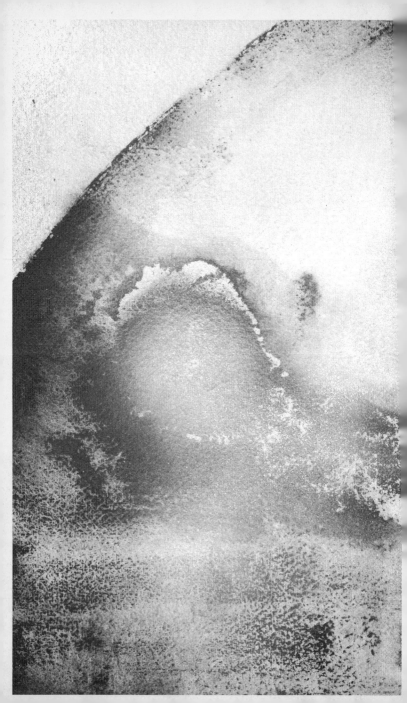

THIS
GREAT ASSEMBLY
OF PEOPLE
WHO LOVE

━━━

Beloved Bhagwan,

A monk asked Seike, "Where does a monk go when he dies and transmigrates?"

Seike said, "The Chōkō flows on and on, never stopping; bubbles obey the vagaries of the wind."

The monk asked further, "Does he receive the ceremonial offerings?"

Seike said, "We can't say there are no ceremonial offerings."

"What exactly are these offerings?" asked the monk.

Seike said, "As the fisherman's song pushes the oar, his voice is heard in the valleys."

Before Chū Kokushi died, emperor Shukusho asked him, "When you are a hundred years old, what shall I do for you?"

Kokushi answered, "Make a seamless pagoda for this old monk."

The emperor said, "I would like to ask you what style is it to be?"

Kokushi remained silent for a while, and then he said, "Do you understand?"

"No, I do not," said the emperor.

"I have a disciple called Tangen," said Kokushi, "who had the dharma seal transmitted by me. He is well versed in this matter. Ask him, please."

After Kokushi's death, the emperor sent for Tangen and asked him about it. Tangen said,

*"South of Shō and north of Tan, in between,
gold abounds.*

*The ferryboat under the shadowless tree, no holy
one in the emerald palace you see."*

Maneesha, this evening and this silence, this
great assembly of people who love is really the
answer to the anecdote you have asked about.
That's what the emperor could not understand
when he asked, "What kind, what style of pagoda,
of temple do you want to be erected?"

The master remained silent. Except silence, what
can represent a Buddha, a Bashō, a Nan-Sen? Only
silence.

I will read the anecdote. Listen as silently as possible because your silence is the answer that has
been raised in the anecdote.

*A monk asked Seike, "Where does a monk go
when he dies and transmigrates?"*

In the first place it is a stupid question because a
man of enlightenment never dies, never transmigrates either. Transmigration is for the ignorant,
from one form into another form, from one animalhood to another animalhood. But for the awakened, for the enlightened there is no death and no
transmigration. He simply defuses into the wholeness of the cosmos.

He does not leave even his steps and their marks
behind him just like a snowflake disappearing or an
echo in the mountains.

He simply drops his bondage and makes the
whole sky his being. He is everywhere and he is
nowhere in particular.

Seike said, "The Chōkō flows" – Chōkō is the
name of a river. *"The Chōkō flows on and on,
never stopping; bubbles obey the vagaries of the*

wind." That's the language Zen prefers, the language of pure poetry, of pure music, of pure dance.

The Chōkō river flows on and on. It has been flowing for centuries or perhaps for millions of years and it will go on flowing; in the same way the enlightened one disappears into the ocean, drops the small cage that he used to think was himself – his personality, his ego. Just like a drop of dew slipping from the lotus leaf and merging into the ocean, he disappears to appear everywhere. You have to risk to be nowhere if you want to be everywhere. But it is a good bargain.

Seike said, "The Chōkō flows on and on, never
stopping; bubbles obey the vagaries of the wind."

Only bubbles go here and there, transmigrate, follow the vagaries of the wind. Fashions and moods and emotions are nothing but soap bubbles. They move from one form into another form, from one place into another place. But the river itself simply continues. Just feel the silent river in which you are at this moment. This silence is eternal: it has always been here and it will always remain here.

The monk asked further, "Does he receive the
ceremonial offerings?"

The monk must have been a super-idiot. He has not heard what Seiko has said. He again repeats the same question from a different angle. "When the master is dead, does he receive the ceremonial offerings?"

Seike said, "We can't say there are no
ceremonial offerings."
"What exactly are these offerings?"
asked the monk.
Seike said, "As the fisherman's song pushes the
oar, his voice is heard in the valleys."

These offerings to the enlightened ones may be

just a few roseflowers. He is asking whether they are received or not. That is not an authentic seeker's question. The question is whether you are offering or not. Those hands which could receive those flowers are no more encaged in flesh, in bones. And when you offer your love, your gratitude will be heard just as the echo of a fisherman's song pushes the oar and his voice is heard in the valleys.

It is difficult to talk about because of the very nature of the phenomenon. Once you become enlightened, you are no longer – in the old sense. You are absolutely discontinuous with the old: the jump is quantum so the old language becomes absolutely inapplicable. All that can be said is: offerings are made; the whole existence receives them; no individual hands are going to receive your offerings.

And the very desire that your offerings should be received is basically wrong: your offerings should be unconditional. They should be out of your love, not out of your desire, not out of any demand. It is just a joy, a dance that a few human beings have disappeared into the cosmic whole.

Your offering is simply a symbolic indication that you would also like to disappear like an echo, slowly, slowly, not leaving any trace behind; just as a bird flies but does not leave footprints in the sky.

Before Chū Kokushi died, emperor Shukusho asked him, "When you are a hundred years old, what shall I do for you?"

Kokushi answered, "Make a seamless pagoda for this old monk."

The emperor said, "I would like to ask you, what style is it to be?"

Kokushi remained silent for a while – this silence was the answer. But only those who are silent can understand the language of silence. Only those whose hearts are present in the moment can dance.

But the emperor could not understand Kokushi and his silence. After a while he said, *"Do you understand?"*

"No, I do not," said the emperor.

"I have a disciple called Tangen," said Kokushi, *"who had the dharma seal transmitted by me. He is well versed in this matter. Ask him, please."*

The emperor has not understood the master because the master will not descend from his silence. He sends him to a disciple.

After Kokushi's death, the emperor sent for Tangen and asked him about it. Tangen said, "South of Shō and north of Tan, in between, gold abounds."

Between these two mountains, gold abounds.

*"The ferryboat under the shadowless tree"...*Just see how Zen is more pictorial than linguistic.

"The ferryboat under the shadowless tree, no holy one in the emerald palace you see."

The anecdote ends because the emperor could not see the heart of silence, the heart of the universal music, the language of the shadows and the poetry of love. But you should not miss. Do you understand? In this silence is the whole secret.

Maneesha has asked:

Beloved Bhagwan,
Whenever I try to die each night – to close down my senses and be dead – I only feel life trying to assert itself more vigorously. Am I doing it wrongly or is that what is meant to happen? Or are there no "meant to happens" here?

Maneesha, it is meant to happen. I am a teacher of life, not of death; but I can teach you only if you are ready even to die for life. Already you are so dead, and still you believe through your whole life that you are alive. But this life is lukewarm. Hence in the meditation I try to help you, to push you deeper into death because as far as I am concerned death is a fiction. The whole intention is that as you try to be more and more dead, you will find life asserting itself.

It is a very deep dialectical process. The more you try to die, the more you will find yourself fresh and young and newly born. I teach resurrection. Jesus should not have the monopoly of being resurrected, it is everybody's right. You don't have to hang on a cross, you can simply die here. You can just leave the body and go in, fearlessly, because there is the eternal treasure of being.

There is no question of losing anything; relax totally so that all energy moves inwards, gathers inwards, becomes a concentrated phenomenon. That's why you are feeling more alive. I want you to be more alive – alive forever, because that is your nature; only recognition is needed.

Meditation is simply a method to recognize the eternity of life and the fiction of death.

This silence is so precious that even the bamboos are not making commentaries today. But I will still give them a little chance to laugh. Laughter dignifies you because no animal laughs. Laughter proves life because dead men don't laugh.

Little Munni Bramachappati, youngest daughter of Mr. and Mrs. Rama Bramachappati, a fifteen-year-old child, is suddenly awakened by deep moaning and groaning coming from the neighbor's flat in "D" building, Popular Heights.

Sleepy-eyed, she goes into her parents' room and

asks, "Mom, what is that noise coming from next door?"

"Don't bother about it, dear," says Mrs. Bramachappati. "That young German lady must have a headache."

Twenty minutes later, little Munni is woken again. "Hey mom," she cries. "It sounds like the young German lady is really suffering now!"

"Just don't bother about it, dear," replies her mother. "She must be having a fever – just go to sleep."

A few minutes later little Munni is woken again. But this time it is a male voice joining in chorus, yelping and roaring, followed by deep silence.

"Mom! Mom! Call the doctor!" cries Munni.

"What is it?" asks Mrs. Bramachappati.

"Well," says Munni, "that poor German girl's fever has just infected that nice American man from downstairs!"

Kowalski goes to stay in a big hotel in Los Angeles for the first time.

"I am not going to have this room," Kowalski complains to the bell-boy. "It is so small I can hardly move in it. It is no better than a pigsty, and I am not going to sleep on that tiny folding bed. Just because I am a Polack, don't think you can fool me!"

"Please get in, sir," says the bell-boy. "This is the elevator!"

Pope the Polack is picked up outside the Vatican on suspicion of rape. He is taken to the police station, finger-printed, booked, and locked in a cell.

A few hours later, he is placed in a line with five other men. He looks around him with some curiosity. There are several cops, some plainclothesmen, and the rape victim. Seeing her, he leaps out of the line and pointing excitedly shouts, "That is her! That is her!"

Mike, the barman at the Dublin Hotel, is thoroughly fed up with Paddy. Every night, Paddy comes in five minutes before closing time, orders three beers and proceeds to drink them very slowly, forcing Mike to stay late. So Mike has an idea. He has heard about Kowalski working as a gorilla, so he goes and asks him to come to the pub that night.

Kowalski waits in the back room in his gorilla suit, and when Mike has served Paddy his three beers, he goes and tells Kowalski to bang his chest, scream and make as much noise as possible. Hearing such frightening noises from the back room the whole pub clears out immediately, except Paddy, who continues sipping his beer.

Then Mike says, "Go out there and really scare him!"

So Kowalski bursts through the door, roaring, banging his chest and jumping up and down. But still Paddy sips his beer. Then Mike shouts, "Get him, gorilla!"

Kowalski leaps over the bar and jumps on Paddy and they roll out of the door, wrestling. Mike can hear a terrible noise of fighting outside, but when it is over, to Mike's horror, Paddy walks in. He is covered in blood and hair, and dusting himself off, sits down and says, "My God! Give a Polack a fur coat and he thinks he owns the place!"

Remember, the first step in meditation is to forget the whole world and just bring out all your craziness in rubbish, gibberish sounds, gestures. But be total because once you are freed of it, then there is a possibility of going deeper into silence than you have ever gone.

The second step will be silence. To make it still deeper, the third step will be falling dead so that your whole life energy shrinks at the center of your being, throbbing and giving you the taste a buddha has every moment.

Rupesh, hit the drum for the first step.

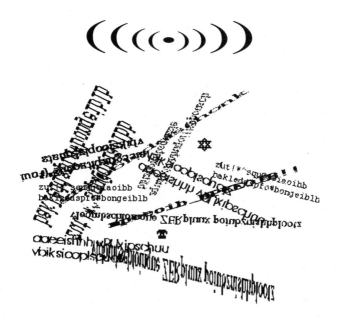

Rupesh…

Be silent, totally silent.
Close your eyes,
no movement.
Just be.

This silence, this moment
is the answer
to all the questions ever asked.

Rupesh, give the third drum.

Fall dead.
Take yourself as deep inwards as possible.
Leave the body, leave the mind.
Take a quantum leap
from mind to no-mind.

No-mind is your very being.

Remember all the buddhas
of the past and future are watching.
Deeper and deeper, fearlessly,
move into the unknown being
of your own existence.

This is what cannot be said in words.
This is where language fails to express.
This evening is blessed
because you are
entering into the innermost temple,
experiencing the ultimate flowering
of your potential.

Rupesh, the drum.

Come back to life,
resurrected, new, fresh.
Don't ever look back.
The whole existence
is now and here.

Okay, Maneesha?
Yes, Bhagwan.
Can we celebrate?
YES!

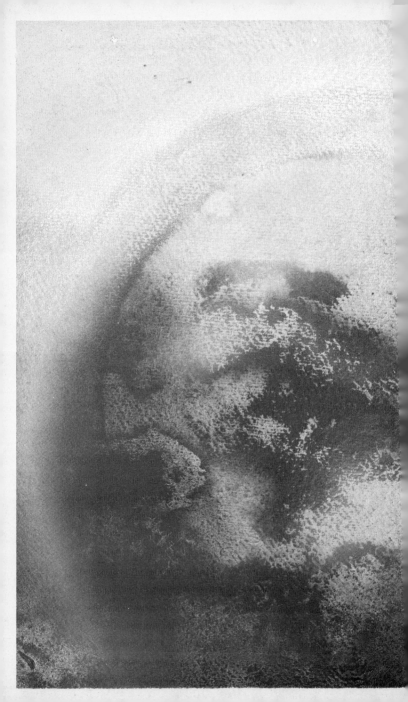

THE BAMBOOS
ARE ASKING FOR
A FEW LAUGHS

Beloved Bhagwan,

An Indian disciple of Enō, Kutta Sanzō, on passing through a village found a monk doing Zazen in a small hut he had built.

Sanzō asked, "What's the idea of sitting here all by yourself?"

The monk answered, "I'm meditating."

Sanzō said, "What is this 'he' who is meditating? What are you meditating on?"

The monk said, "I don't know what you're getting at."

Sanzō said, "Why don't you look at yourself, and quieten yourself?"

The monk still looked blank.

Sanzō then asked him, "What school are you of?"

"Jinshū's," said the monk.

Sanzō said, "Even the lowest heretics in the India I come from don't fall as low as that! Just to sit emptily and aimlessly – what can it profit you?"

One day, Yakusan was doing Zazen. Sekitō asked him, "What are you doing?"

"Not a thing," replied Yakusan.

"Aren't you sitting blankly?" said Sekitō.

"If I were sitting blankly, I would be doing something," retorted Yakusan.

Sekitō said, "Tell me, what is that which you are not doing?"

Yakusan replied, "A thousand sages could not answer that question."

The attendant, O, together with Rinzai,
entered the hall. O asked, "Do these monks
read the sutras?"

"Not they!" replied Rinzai.

"Then they're learning Zen?" asked attendant O.

"No," replied Rinzai.

"Then what on earth are they all up to?" asked O.

"They're busy becoming buddhas,"
said Rinzai, "becoming patriarchs."

O said, "Gold dust is valuable but in the eye
it is injurious."

Rinzai said, "I thought you were just
a mediocre person!"

Maneesha, the anecdote before me needs to be understood against a certain background.

It is very sad that Gautam Buddha was born in this country, but was not understood by this country. His message was so deep, so inward, so existential that the Indian heritage of thousands of years of learning, scholarship, philosophy, theology, religion, all became a barrier. Of course a few people understood Gautam Buddha, but very few. Just three hundred years after Gautam Buddha died, Alexander the Great came to India and his historians record they could not find a single enlightened Buddhist.

Buddhism has been destroyed by the brahmins, the pandits and the scholars, the intellectuals of this country, because Buddha's message was not intellectual. Thousands of Buddhists left the country, were driven out, killed or burned, but within just three hundred years not even the foot-prints of the greatest man that has lived in this land were left. Those who escaped alive reached

China, Tibet, Korea, Taiwan, Japan, all over Asia.

It is a strange and sad story that India gave birth to one of the greatest men of the world, but the mediocre masses of India could not understand him. The distance was too much. The distance was between the mind and no-mind: Gautam Buddha is a quantum leap. He does not teach you any theology, he simply wants you to be, neither doing, nor non-doing, but just being. He has no God to preach to you, no rituals to be followed; he is the first man in the world to make freedom of being the ultimate right of every living creature.

Obviously the very ancient tradition of Indian scholarship could not tolerate him. In his presence a few blessed ones drank as deeply from his well as possible; but as his body was dead, his last incarnation was finished and he became a part of the total existence. India goes on proclaiming itself the land of Gautam Buddha without seeing the point that they killed him. Of course they killed him with sophistication, not like Jews crucifying Jesus or Greeks poisoning Socrates; they did it in a more subtle way: by not understanding him.

The anecdote has to be understood against this background.

An Indian disciple of Enō, Kutta Sanzō, on passing through a village found a monk doing Zazen in a small hut he had built.

Zazen means just being, neither doing something, nor not doing anything, an utter silence.

Sanzō asked, "What is the idea of sitting here all by yourself?"

It is not only Sanzō; it has been asked by this whole country and it is being asked today by the whole world. The question is significant, *"What is the idea of sitting here all by yourself?"*

The monk answered, "I'm meditating."

Now, before entering into the anecdote more deeply, you have to understand that there is no word which can translate Zazen. 'Meditation' is just a faraway echo, because a word is needed only if a certain experience requires it. In the English language there are three words: 'concentration', 'contemplation', 'meditation', but all three words point to an object. You can ask, "On what are you concentrating?" "What are you contemplating?" "On what are you meditating?"

Zazen comes from the Sanskrit root *dhyan*. Gautam Buddha did not use Sanskrit to make his existential statement – Sanskrit is the language of the scholar; it has never been the language of the people – He chose to speak in the language of the people amongst whom he was born. The name of the language he used is Pali. In Pali the Sanskrit *dhyan* becomes *jhan*.

It happens in every language: the scholars, the rabbis, the roshis, the pandits speak a language with perfection, although their language is dead. But nothing can remain perfect. As the language comes to the people – living people – it becomes more rounded, it changes. *Dhyan* becomes *jhan;* and because the Buddhists, through Bodhidharma and others, reached China…*jhan* turned into *ch'an*.

Words move from one language into another and then take a different shape and color from what was originally theirs. So when *ch'an* reached Japan, it became *zen*. This zen is not translatable, because it is not concentrating on anything, it is not contemplating anything, it is not even meditating on anything; it is just being – a subjective experience without any object.

We use the word 'meditation' in a very arbitrary

way, because there is no other word in English. But you have to understand that we are giving meditation a totally new meaning, which it does not have in the English language. It cannot, because the West has never entered into subjectivity; it has been continuously concerned with the objective. *That* has been its concern, not *this;* the faraway has been its concern, but not the obvious; the other has been its concern, but not oneself.

So when the monk – remember he is an Indian, his name must have been changed into Japanese – Kutta Sanzō immediately asked, *"What is the idea of sitting here by yourself?"*

The monk answered, "I'm meditating."

Sanzō said, "What is this 'he' who is meditating? What are you meditating on?"

The very questions, *"What are you meditating on?", "What is this 'he' who is meditating?"...* In these small questions, both the Western attitude and the Indian attitude are expressed together, but not the approach of Gautam Buddha. The moment he is sitting silently, doing nothing, the Hindu thinks he has found the soul, the self. The West simply has not tried sitting silently.

The West has found great truths about the objective world, but not even a small shadow of the inner. In fact it denies the inner. It is extraordinary to accept the outer and to deny the inner. It is illogical and absurd: the outer can be outer only if there is something inner; if there is nobody inside you, do you think anything will be outside you? You are the world, because your consciousness is there; it reflects the whole world around you. But the West has been denying consistently the inner self. Their reasons are that the inner self does not fulfill scientific requirements.

It is just like asking a blind man about light, or a deaf person about music. Naturally the blind man can say, "I don't see any light anywhere; light does not exist, because it does not fulfill my requirements." That's what science has been doing. It is imposing its requirements, which are inapplicable to the inner... They are perfectly good for the outer. Just because the blind man cannot see the sun, the sun does not disappear, and just because the deaf person cannot hear, it does not mean there is no sound, no music. Just because you are focused on the outside, it does not mean that the inner is non-existential.

The West has committed one mistake, denying subjectivity, denying consciousness. India has committed another mistake by making the inner also just like an object, a self-realization, *atma.* Gautam Buddha is perhaps the first revolutionary of the world who says, "The inner is not a person, the inner is only an eternal living space." Perhaps he is the only man who has asserted the truth.

The man, *the monk who was meditating, said,*
"I don't know what you are getting at."
Sanzō said, "Why don't you look at yourself,
and quieten yourself?"
The monk still looked blank.
Sanzō then asked him, "What school are you of?"
Sanzō seems to be an intellectual belonging to a certain school of philosophy, religion, theology. The monk's silence is not understood.

The monk said, *"Jinshū's." Sanzō said,*
"Even the lowest heretics in the India I come
from don't fall as low as that! Just to sit emptily
and aimlessly – what can it profit you?"
India could not understand Gautam Buddha for this simple reason. They think that to sit silently,

just being, is worthless. You have to do something, you have to pray, you have to recite mantras, you have to go to some temple and worship a man-made god. "What are you doing sitting silently?"

And that is the greatest contribution of Gautam Buddha, that you can find your eternity and your cosmic being only if you can sit silently, aimlessly, without any desire and without any longing, just enjoying being the silent space in which thousands of lotuses blossom.

Gautam Buddha is a category in himself. Very few people have understood him. Even in the countries where Buddhism is a national religion, Thailand, Japan, Taiwan, it has become an intellectual philosophy. Zazen, the original contribution of the man, has disappeared. Perhaps you are the people who are the closest contemporaries of Gautam Buddha at this moment. In this silence, in this emptiness, in this quantum leap from mind to no-mind you have entered a different space, which is neither outer nor inner, but transcendental to both.

One day, Yakusan was doing Zazen.
Sekitō asked him, "What are you doing?"
"Not a thing," replied Yakusan.
"Are not you sitting blankly?" said Sekitō
"If I were sitting blankly, I would be doing
something."

Do you see the point? Do you understand this tremendous answer, *"If I were sitting blankly, I would be* doing *something,"* retorted Yakusan.

Sekitō said, "Tell me, what is that which you are
not doing?"
Yakusan replied, "A thousand sages could not
answer that question."

Yakusan is right and wrong. Yakusan is right: it is

true, a thousand buddhas cannot say anything about the transcendental. But I say also that Yakusan is *not* right, because a thousand buddhas here can experience it; there is no need to say anything.

This blessed evening we are entering into the transcendental. Now remember these three words: the outer, which has become a fixation in the West, the inner, which has become a fixation of the Indian mind, and the transcendental, which is the message of the awakened ones. They don't belong to any country, they don't belong to any race, they don't belong to any school of philosophy, they simply belong to existence itself.

Those who have gathered here are no longer objective, no longer subjective, but just drowning into the transcendental.

The transcendental is the only truth,
beyond division, beyond duality,
only a pure sky,
a fragrance that you cannot hold in your hands,
a silence that dances in your heart,
a peace that passeth understanding.

And you cannot say a single word about it. Yakusan has to forgive me saying that he is both right and wrong. Right because a thousand sages could not answer that question, and wrong because just a single buddha is the answer. The answer will not be materialized into language. But it can be experienced, and unless you experience it, you will have wasted your life absolutely.

The attendant, O, together with Rinzai,
entered the hall. O asked, "Do these monks
read the sutras?"
"Not they!" replied Rinzai.
"Then they are learning Zen?"
asked attendant O.

"No," replied Rinzai.
"Then what on earth are they all up to?" asked O.
"They are busy becoming buddhas,"
said Rinzai, "becoming patriarchs."
O said, "Gold dust is valuable but in the eye
it is injurious."
Rinzai said, "I thought you were just
a mediocre person!"

Rinzai is a great master and what he is saying is true, that his understanding about the questioner was not right; he had thought him a mediocre person.

But I want to say that even if a man is a genius as far as mind is concerned, it does not make any difference; the mediocre and the genius, both are within the mind, and the truth is beyond.

I have unfortunately to correct Rinzai. The man may not have been mediocre, but he was not the man of Zen, he was not in the dimension of the transcendental, which is the only truth there is. Everything else is nothing but soap bubbles.

Maneesha has asked,

Beloved Bhagwan
Does the mind only continue to dominate us because of our need to control? It seems to me that all our loveliest moments in life are those experiences when we feel out of control, taken over, obliterated. Yet we continually turn down the invitation to be in that space twenty-four hours a day.

Maneesha, it is true that your most precious moments are those when you are not, when you are obliterated. And your understanding is correct that you continue to hold to the mind because mind gives you the capacity to control. Mind is aggressive. Even in moments when it is not needed, it goes on insisting on control.

For example in love, what is the need of the mind? But it *grabs,* it wants to control, it is afraid; perhaps if it does not control, the person may move away. And the strange story is, the more you try to control, the more you are destroying the very fact of love.

Love can blossom only when not controlled, when nothing is asked and demanded; then it opens up to its fullest flowering, fills the whole sky with its fragrance. But you cannot have love in your fist. Even air disappears from your fist, and man has lived up to now as a fist!

I teach the open hand. Zen is the open hand: don't control, do not demand and all is yours; all the stars and all the flowers and all the oceans and all that existence can give is yours. But *you* should not be; you should be simply a space, an open hand.

Maneesha, you may be getting a little intellectual understanding, but existential understanding you cannot lose – it is once and for all, once forever. Then you cannot say that we forget who we are. You are obliterated; who is there to forget it? You are no more, you are filled with the whole, twenty-four hours, from eternity to eternity. There is no forgetfulness; but if it is only intellectual understanding then you are bound to forget it.

Here every day you enter into the eternal, you experience it, you rejoice and dance in it. And again you are back in the mind which has never given you anything but misery.

Before we enter into the transcendental, the poor bamboos are asking for a few laughs.

Mike and Paddy are sitting around drinking a few beers.

"How is your wife looking these days?" Mike asks Paddy.

"She went to the beauty shop and got a mud pack," replies Paddy, "and for two days she looked nice. Then the mud fell off."

Do you see, Maneesha? This is not a joke, but a Zen story.

Dr. Ekdam Kwality is feeling that his private practice has been going slowly lately, when in walks Swami Herschel with stomach cramps.

"Oh dear," says the doctor. "I am afraid I will have to operate."

"What! Really?" cries Swami Herschel. "Surgery for amoebas?"

"Yes, yes, don't be worried – it is very common," says the doctor. "It will only cost twenty thousand rupees."

"What! Really?" cries Herschel again. "Twenty thousand rupees for gas pains? I can't afford *that!*"

"You *can* afford it," insists Dr. Ekdam Kwality. "Just put down five thousand rupees now and then it is just one thousand rupees a month for the next two years."

"My God!" exclaims Herschel. "You make it sound like buying a car!"

Dr. Ekdam Kwality looks astonished and asks, "How did you know I was buying a car?"

Pope the Polack goes into the optician's and says, "I need a new pair of glasses."

"I knew that," replies the optician, "as soon as you walked in through the window."

Swami Deva Coconut is on the way to M.G. Road on his motorbike, when he is hit by a runaway bullock cart. As luck would have it, he lands up in heaven. After a few days rest, he asks for some work. Finally, he is given a job in the Religious Statistics Department.

Here they have a clock for every religious leader on earth, and any sins committed by them are recorded by a tiny movement forward. The pope's clock has moved only two minutes in sixty-eight years, Mother Teresa's clock only one minute, and so on.

Swami Coconut enquires of the angel in charge, "What about Bhagwan's clock?"

"Oh," cries the angel. "We use his clock as a desk fan!" – twenty-four hours!"

Now, Rupesh, give the first beat and everybody goes crazy…

Rupesh…

Everybody goes into silence; close your eyes;
gather yourself in. Just be.
This is the message
of the thousand buddhas;
it cannot be said, only experienced.
Go deeper.

Rupesh, give the beat and everybody falls dead…

Your body can go on breathing, but you go on
and on beyond the mind into a clearance
where there is just open space, not even you!
Just pure silence!
What Yakusan could not say,
five thousand buddhas are experiencing
in this moment.
Go as deep as possible,
don't be afraid.
It is your own being, unknown,
unexperienced, unexplored.
Open your wings and fly like an eagle
across the sun.
Drink deep, nourish yourself
with this transcendental experience
so that it becomes
your twenty-four hour breathing.

Rupesh, give the beat…

Come back to life.
Resurrect, fresh, young, alive,
having no past, no future,
having no body, no mind.
Just be.
This is your authentic existence.
Except this, all philosophy,
metaphysics is nothing but nonsense.

Okay, Maneesha?
Yes, Bhagwan.
Can we now celebrate the evening?
YES!

START LIVING
IN A POEM

—

Beloved Bhagwan,

One day, while Nan-Sen was living in a little hut in the mountains, a strange monk visited him just as he was preparing to go to his work in the fields.

Nan-Sen welcomed him, saying, "Please make yourself at home. Cook anything you like for your lunch, then bring some of the leftover food to me along the road leading to my work place."

Nan-Sen worked hard until evening, and came home very hungry. The stranger had cooked and enjoyed a good meal by himself, then thrown away all provisions and broken all the utensils. Nan-Sen found the monk sleeping peacefully in the empty hut, but when he stretched his own tired body beside the stranger's, the latter got up and went away.

Years later, Nan-Sen told the anecdote to his disciples, with the comment, "He was such a good monk – I miss him even now."

Maneesha, Zen is anything but unkindness, but ungracefulness. It is pure compassion. And compassion is tested only when you think it is almost impossible to be compassionate.

This small anecdote about a great Zen master, Nan-Sen, has tremendous implications for you all to understand – not only intellectually , but with your whole being. Feel the meaning in every cell of your body, mind and soul. It would be very difficult to find such a story in the history of any other religion.

One day, while Nan-Sen was living in a little hut in the mountains, a strange monk visited him just as he was preparing to go to his work in the fields.

Each and every word has to be understood clearly. A stranger is not accepted by people. Just his being strange creates fear in you, because he is unpredictable. Leaving his hut to work in the field, telling this strange man to rest, needs immense trust, a trust that even if betrayed, cannot be destroyed.

He did not even ask the name of the monk nor from where he came, nor what was his purpose, what he wanted from him. No question at all... Such is the approach of Zen – no question at all, but a deep acceptance of the strangeness of everything.

All this is symbolic. Do you know the bamboos outside Buddha Hall? Do you know these people and the clouds that pass over and the rain? Everything is strange and that is the beauty of it. Just as the bamboos and the flowers and the roses and the clouds and the stars are accepted without their names, their caste, their country, their race, the same should be the approach to human beings. Why do you discriminate? Why do you ask a human being his name, his purpose? You do it so you can drop your fear of the stranger.

In fact, everybody is a stranger, even your wife or your husband or your children. Do you know your children? They are as much strangers as the bamboos or perhaps even more, because they come from you but they are not from you – they come from the beyond. Yet you did not ask the child, "Why have you come?"

That is the approach of Zen. Nan-Sen did not ask the strange monk. On the contrary, he *welcomed him, saying, "Please make yourself at home."*

In a small anecdote, in a few words the very essence can be expressed. "Make yourself at home."

156

A man like Nan-Sen does not possess anything: the whole existence is his home; this small hut cannot confine him, cannot become his possession.

He said to the stranger, *"Please make yourself at home. Cook anything you like for your lunch, then bring some of the leftover food to me along the road leading to my work place."*

Do you see? He is not saying, "Prepare my lunch." He is saying, "Prepare your lunch and if something is left over, bring it to me in the field where I will be working."

Nan-Sen worked hard until evening, and came home very hungry. The stranger had cooked and enjoyed a good meal by himself, then thrown away all provisions and broken all the utensils. Nan-Sen found the monk sleeping peacefully in the empty hut, but when he stretched his own tired body beside the stranger's, the latter got up and went away.

Even then, Nan-Sen did not ask what had happened to the leftover food. He did not ask, "Where are all the utensils? And where are you going?" A non-questioning attitude towards existence, a pure innocent acceptance that the stranger must be doing whatever he feels right to do.

Years later, Nan-Sen told the anecdote to his disciples, with the comment, "He was such a good monk – I miss him even now."

This is the very essence of compassion, of love, of trust. You cannot betray it: by betraying it, you are betraying yourself. That strange monk had done everything to destroy Nan-Sen's trust in humanity. But on the contrary, Nan-Sen's trust has passed through a fire test.

Years later he said, "He was such a good monk – I miss him even now."

If you can understand the approach of no conditions, no judgement... There was every possibility that Nan-Sen would have judged that, "The fellow proved absolutely unworthy of my trust." Then the trust is very small; Nan-Sen's trust is as big as the whole sky. What harm did he do? Of course he missed a meal, his utensils are broken, but these are small things. Only mediocre minds care about these things. People who have an inner richness, who know their kingdom of God, will not be bothered by such things. "That fellow must have his own reasons; who am I to judge? At least he did not kill me. He did not burn down the hut. He was such a good fellow," Nan-Sen says. *I miss him even now* – his generosity, his peace, his silently moving away without bothering me."

Compassion can be only unlimited. If you put a limit on your compassion, you are deceiving yourself because beyond the limit, doubt is waiting. Beyond the limit begins the distrust. What harm has he done that you should lose a precious experience of trust? In fact, he has given an opportunity to Nan-Sen to see for himself that he is not angry, that he is not suspicious, that his compassion is not limited. He is thankful to the stranger and later on he says, *"He was such a good monk – I miss him even now."*

If you can experience the point, your whole life will be transformed. Then this whole existence is no longer strange, it becomes very familiar. You are at home everywhere. Nobody, not even animals, birds, this cuckoo, these silently standing bamboos...they all become friends. You start living in poetry, you start living in a dance which knows no doubt.

Religion has been giving a false coin to people called belief. If you look in the dictionaries, belief and trust and faith seem to be synonymous. They are not: belief is always belief in some hypothesis; faith is always out of fear; trust has a totally different quality – it is out of understanding, out of love. Once you start living out of love, only then do you know what religion is. Zen is the purest form of religion.

Maneesha has asked:

Beloved Bhagwan,
Is this a story about a master's compassion and equanimity in the face of his trust being abused? Or is it a beautiful illustration of benefitting from being with a master without being needy and dependent? Certainly, it is Your voice I hear when I read Nan-Sen's saying: "He was such a good monk – I miss him even now."

Maneesha, Nan-Sen has missed only one good monk. I have missed thousands whom I have loved, whom I have trusted and who have not only broken my utensils and spoilt one of my meals. They have broken everything they could, they have burnt my heart. Still, I miss them.

Just today I heard that one of my sannyasins has written a book, condemning the whole experiment here. The book was published two and a half years ago, and it came to my notice today because the sannyasin, a woman, a beautiful woman with a very nice heart, has informed me that she is coming in September.

In the book, she wrote, "I was naive, childish. That's why I became a disciple. Now I am mature and absolutely free from sannyas." I wonder why she is coming back. But if she comes back, nobody should ask her a single question about the book,

about the lies that she has spoken in it. It is all past. In two and a half years, so much water has gone down the Ganges. Who bothers? Even if you only come back home in the evening, having gone astray here and there, you are welcome.

Thousands of sannyasins have betrayed – not me, themselves – for trivia. The American government has bribed a few people to say things which are absolutely untrue because for three and a half years I was silent. Those people have confessed to the government that I arranged their marriage. I have not been able to arrange my own marriage and I don't think now there is any possibility. Why should I bother about arranging anybody else's marriage? And I had not seen those people, I don't remember their faces. I never even talked with them, because for three and a half years I was silent. And even when I am speaking, I am speaking publicly: I don't see people individually.

Marriage is their personal affair. If anything, I can arrange for the divorce, not for the marriage. That is my whole philosophy – divorce! But those two sannyasins got a big enough bribe and were ready to tell the court that I had arranged their marriage. I have not said anything. Even if they come back, they will be welcomed, although I have been dragged because of them from jail to jail, poisoned because of them and fined half a million dollars.

And I don't have a single dollar; I have not even seen the face of a single dollar. I have not touched money for almost thirty years. I don't know who paid the fine. Of course, sannyasins were so much hurt that within ten minutes half a million dollars were paid. Even the judge could not believe his eyes. They were thinking that that much money I will not be able…. I had nothing.

And those who betray are not few, but many. Those to whom I gave respect and love – and still I love them – have done everything to harm my approach to life. They are afraid even to mention that they have been with me.

Just the other day, I received a brochure from Swami Anand Teertha whom twelve sannyasins have joined to make a therapist team. Anand Teertha, who lived with me here for thirteen years, writes in his introduction that he has been with an Indian mystic for thirteen years. He has not the courage even to say who this Indian mystic is – do you hear? Even the cuckoo is more understanding – Teertha's wife certainly has more courage than Teertha; at least she mentions my name, that she was learning under me as my disciple for thirteen years.

Teertha could not prevent her because she is no longer with him. He is living with another woman, a girlfriend. That girlfriend was also here. She also does not mention...again comes the Indian mystic. But if they come back, they will receive the same love. I don't take note of such stupid fears. What is their fear? Their fear is that my name makes them harassed by governments. They cannot work in Germany or in Italy if the governments knows that they have been my people.

But selling your soul so cheap...I have only tears for them. And now, they themselves are closing the door. From my side it is open, but the things they are saying to other sannyasins: "Drop sannyas. It is dangerous. Twenty-one countries have passed laws that Bhagwan cannot enter. Your job is at risk."

And it is true. A few teachers have lost their jobs. A professor has lost his job because he accepted me as his master. But he was a courageous man. He went to the court and asked, "Is there any law that prevents me from being a disciple of Bhagwan? Is it in any way a hindrance to my teaching in the college? I have not been teaching his philosophy; I am not even capable of teaching it. But my association with him has taken away my job."

There are almost two million sannyasins in the world. I have told them not to wear orange clothes, not to wear the mala, because I don't want anyone to suffer because of me. But anybody trying to persuade sannyasins to drop sannyas... Now what is left as far as sannyas is concerned? I have told them to forget about the orange clothes, throw away their malas in the ocean. Only meditation is the essence. Just keep to it, nobody can even suspect that you are a meditator. It is your inner, innermost center.

Maneesha, it is both. The story is "a master's compassion and equanimity in the face of his trust being abused." And it is also "a beautiful illustration of benefitting from being with a master without being needy and dependent."

Yes, Maneesha, certainly it is my voice that you have heard in Nan-Sen's saying, *"He was such a good monk – I miss him even now."* You don't know, perhaps nobody else in the world has missed as many people as I have missed. I am carrying wounds from the hands of my own people; but my love is as alive as ever, because it was never dependent on what they do. It was never conditional; it is simply that I love, I am love. So whoever comes close to me can drink the nectar of love and silence and peace. I don't make any demand that you have to fulfill. I am just like an open sky.

Maneesha has asked another question, too:

Beloved Bhagwan,
Does a disciple need to need her master and to be conscious of needing him?

No, Maneesha. Need is not the language of Zen: love is the language. You need things but – it is a strange and insane world – people love things. Somebody loves a car, somebody loves a horse, somebody loves a rented bicycle. In this insane world people need each other and reduce each other into things. The moment you need someone, you have taken away the dignity of that person. You have reduced him into a commodity.

In India, the woman is called *stridhan,* feminine wealth. And when a girl gets married, the word that is used is *dana,* donation. These are ugly words; you cannot donate a person, you cannot purchase a person. It is only in theory that we think slavery has disappeared from the world. It exists in thousands of ways, with different faces.

At least don't ask a master to be needed, and anybody worth his salt, if he is a master, does not need a disciple. He loves to share and he is grateful to all those who are receptive. Neither is the disciple a need nor is the master a need. Need is a word applicable to things. Here in this temple, all are loved; nobody is needed. And the difference has to be understood: need becomes a prison and love is freedom; need puts chains on you and love gives you wings.

The bamboos are whispering amongst themselves. They want a little laughter.

Little Ernie's parents have invited the local Protestant priest and his wife to tea. Ernie has been told to be on his best behavior, and to say "Please" and "Thank you" at all times. But Ernie is having trouble, and by the end of the afternoon is almost ready to burst.

"Would you like some more tea, Ernest?" asks his mother.

"No!" says Ernie.

"No *what*, dear?" asks his mother, with a threatening look. She prompts him again, "No *what?*"

To which Ernie replies, "No more fucking tea!"

Stanley Sharkskin, the traveling salesman, is too tired to continue his journey in the dark country night. He sees a little farmhouse by the side of the road and decides to seek some comfort and rest there.

"Can you put me up for the night?" Stanley asks the farmer.

"Sure, but you will have to sleep with my son," says the farmer.

"My God!" exclaims Stanley, "I am in the wrong joke!"

It is evening in a bar in New York. A young, long-haired boy, with a guitar and a high-pitched nasal voice, is singing "My Old California Home." An old man in the corner bows down his head and quietly weeps.

A lady sitting near him leans over and says, "Excuse me, old timer, but are you a Californian?"

"No, lady," sobs the man. "I'm a musician."

"Have faith and you shall be healed," cries the preacher at the revival meeting. A woman on crutches and a man come forward. The preacher asks, "What is your name, my good woman?"

"I'm Mrs. Smith," she replies, "and I have had

to walk with crutches all my life."

"Well, Mrs. Smith," says the preacher, "go behind that screen and pray."

Turning to the man, he asks, "What is your name?"

"My name ith Thamuelth," he replies, "and I have alwayth thpoken with a lithp."

"Alright, Mr. Samuels," says the preacher, "go behind that screen with Mrs. Smith, and pray!"

Then the preacher raises his arms and says, "Witness the miracles! Mrs. Smith, throw one crutch over the screen." The audience gasps as it sails over. "Mrs. Smith," cries the preacher. "Now the other one!" The crowd cheers as the second crutch appears. Encouraged, the preacher commands, "Mr. Samuels, say something in a loud, clear voice."

Samuels answers, "Mithuth Thmith jutht fell on her arth!"

Rupesh, give the first drum and everybody goes crazy. Nothing less will do.

Rupesh...

Everybody becomes silent.
Close your eyes
and gather your energy inwards.
No movement. Just be.
A single-pointed consciousness
and you have taken the quantum leap
from mind to no-mind.
Deeper, deeper. There is no fear, go deeper.
It is lonely, it is silent
but it is immensely blissful.
This is the lotus
the buddhas have been talking about.
This is the secret that can be indicated
but cannot be explained.
At this moment
you are at the very heartbeat of existence.
Let it become your very life-style.
With it comes a tremendous spring
of life, of joy, of blessings, of love.
It is a dance which is multi-dimensional.
Every creativity comes out of this space:
poetry, music, sculpture...
all that is great is born through this womb,
the womb of inner silence.
Make it deeper.

Rupesh, give another beat for everyone to die.

Just let the body breathe,
but you go on and on inwards.
This is the sacred temple of your being.
Out of it arises every virtue and if you forget it,
your life is meaningless.
A thousand and one roses
blossom in this silence.
If you forget it, your life is just a drag
from the cradle to the grave.
It is all up to you
whether you want to live in a desert
or in a garden,
whether you want to be just bones
and a skeleton
or a divine consciousness.

Rupesh, give the beat so that all those who have
died can come back to life.

Resurrect,
but don't forget the moment you have been in
and don't forget
the space that you have traveled.
Don't forget that nothing is more precious
than your own being.
This remembrance
makes each one of you a buddha.

Okay, Maneesha?
Yes, Bhagwan.
Can we celebrate with so many buddhas?
YES!

ZEN IS NOT
A RETAIL SHOP –
IT IS WHOLESALE

Beloved Bhagwan,

Suigan, thinking he had attained something of Zen, left Jimyō's monastery, when he was still a young monk, to travel all over China.

Years later, when Suigan returned to visit the monastery, his old teacher asked, "Tell me the summary of Buddhism."

Suigan answered, "If a cloud does not hang over the mountain, the moonlight will penetrate the waves of the lake."

Jimyō looked at his former pupil in anger. He said, "You are getting old! Your hair has turned white, and your teeth are sparse, yet you still have such an idea of Zen. How can you escape birth and death?"

Tears washed Suigan's face as he bent his head. After a few minutes he asked, "Please tell me the summary of Buddhism."

"If a cloud does not hang over the mountain," the teacher replied, "the moonlight will penetrate the waves of the lake."

Before the teacher had finished speaking, Suigan was enlightened.

Maneesha, enlightenment is an instantaneous awareness, understanding; it has nothing to do with rational, philosophical, or theological mind. It is just a gesture, not a word. It is here, this very moment, the very essence of Zen.

This is a beautiful anecdote, particularly for this evening, when there is so much silence and the birds are singing and the bamboos are listening silently. Such moments cannot be reduced to language and the moment you reduce them, you destroy them. They are always virgin; that is their very essence.

Suigan, thinking he had attained something of Zen...

Remember, it is very easy to think that you have attained something of Zen. But thinking has nothing to do with Zen. It is the barrier. If you think you have attained something of Zen, you have missed. Zen is a non-thinking, silent rejoicing within yourself, a dance of consciousness without any boundaries of words, thoughts.

Suigan was wrong from the very beginning when he thought that he had attained something of Zen. Secondly, Zen is not possible to be attained in installments. It is absolutely un-American. Either you have it in its wholeness or you don't have it. But in parts, it is not available. Nothing can be done about it: this is the very nature of things.

So on both counts he was wrong. First, he thought, and Zen is beyond thinking; second, he thought that he had got something of Zen. You cannot get something of Zen. It never comes in parts and pieces: it is not a retail shop, it is wholesale. When it comes, it comes so totally that it leaves no space for any thought.

But *Suigan, thinking he had attained something of Zen left Jimyō's monastery,* his master. These anecdotes are being lived here again. We are not reading them, we are living them; there is no other way to understand them.

There are many sannyasins who have left, thinking they have attained something. Suigan is only symbolic. Somendra thinks he has attained something, Rajen thinks he has attained something. And there are many Somendras and many Rajens.

Don't belong to that category any of you, because it is very easy for the mind to persuade you that you have attained it. Then you think, "What am I doing here?" Remember this, when your mind says, "My God, in what unknown space have I entered? I cannot figure out what it is – a taste, a sweetness, a fragrance, a joy, a song without words, a music without any instruments."

The old Chinese proverb is: 'When the musician becomes perfect, he throws away his instruments. When the archer becomes perfect, he forgets about his bow and his arrows'. When a meditator comes to his very center, there is a dance, an immense blissfulness overflooding him, but there is no thought. Beware of thinking. That is your enemy number one.

Suigan, thinking he had attained something of Zen, left Jimyō's monastery, when he was still a young monk, to travel all over China.
Years later, when Suigan returned to visit the monastery, his old master asked,
"Tell me the summary of Buddhism."

These kinds of questions are very special to Zen: they don't say what you hear; they don't mean what you understand; they are only indications. Asking, *"Tell me the summary of Buddhism,"* he is not asking like a professor. Anybody can summarize, any scholar can do it. The master is not asking for the summary of Buddhism, he is asking you to show your understanding, "Have you arrived home? Have you got it?"

Suigan answered, and he missed again. This was the time; if he had remained silent, just open and available to the master, he would have instantaneously become the very summary of Buddhism, the very summary of existence. But he answered. Zen is not a question-answer thing. You cannot answer in words: only silence can give the proof that you have understood. But he could not remain silent.

He answered, *"If a cloud does not hang over the mountain, the moonlight will penetrate the waves of the lake."*

Jimyō looked at his former pupil in anger. He said, "You are getting old! Your hair has turned white, and your teeth are sparse, yet you still have such an idea of Zen. How can you escape birth and death?"

Escaping from birth and death is a way of describing the entrance into the transcendental which is never born and never dies.

Tears washed Suigan's face as he bent his head. After a few minutes he asked,

"Please tell me the summary of Buddhism."

The master said, *"If a cloud does not hang over the mountain, the moonlight will penetrate the waves of the lake."*

The beauty is that the same answer was given by Suigan. It was not right and now it is right. What is said does not matter, but from what source, from what understanding, from what silence.

Suigan was simply repeating like a puppet. That answer is written in so many sutras. It was not his own. That's why the master was angry, angry out of compassion, angry because, *"You are getting old!* How are you going to manage not to be born again? Time is so short and you are still a parrot."

All pundits, all roshis, all professors, all rabbis, all popes are just parrots! And they do such immense harm to humanity that it is incalculable.

Just a few days ago the Shankaracharya of Puri – I'm an old, intimate enemy of his – asked the Indian government that the ancient *sati pratha* should be legalized! For centuries Hinduism has been forcing women, when their husbands die, to jump into the funeral pyres, alive, to be burned and die.

This is called *sati*. The word *sati* comes from *sat*, 'the truth'. Calling a woman *sati* because she has jumped into the funeral pyre of her husband is saying that she has attained the truth. If this is true, then why has not a single man in the whole of history jumped into the funeral pyre of his wife? Such an easy way to become one with truth! At least the Shankaracharya of Puri should commit sati. That would make his name history, the only man in the whole of history... And he is such an idiot, he can do it! It is good that he should; otherwise, he has no right to ask the government.

Hindus have been torturing women for centuries. If somebody, out of love, jumps into the funeral pyre – whether it is man or woman does not matter, if it comes out of love – then I have tremendous respect for it. But it was not coming out of love, it was being forced.

If a woman did not commit suicide, she had to live her whole life without getting married again. The rule does not apply to men. Once their wife dies, they immediately start looking around for someone else to possess. The women who jumped were forced to jump. And the way it used to happen...the woman was dragged along, great drums were beaten so nobody could hear her crying; a great quantity of *ghee* – purified butter – was poured on the funeral pyre, creating so much smoke, nobody could see what was happening to the poor woman.

And if any woman resisted and was powerful enough or rich enough and the Hindu priesthood could not manage to force her to commit suicide, she was condemned for her whole life like a servant: she had to shave her hair, she could not wear any ornament; she could only use white clothes, without any color; she could not participate in any religious festivals; she could not even participate in somebody's marriage; she could not be present at somebody's birth. She was simply thrown out of all ceremonials, she had to live like a shadow in the servants' quarters behind the house.

This was much more painful than just to take a jump into the funeral pyre, when it would be finished within minutes. So every intelligent woman, rather than living for sixty years or seventy years in utter slavery and condemnation, chose to commit suicide. It is not sati!

And this fellow, the Shankaracharya of Puri, was speaking on the occasion where a six-year-old girl – in fact it is illegal for her even to be married – was burned on the funeral pyre of her husband. Nor was she of an age to be married. Their marriage was invalid, illegal, unconstitutional and this murder is supported by the Shankaracharya of Puri.

On this occasion he was asking the government to make *sati pratha* legal. I am asking the Indian government to make it a law that every shankaracharya should commit sati first. There are eight shankaracharyas in India. Only after that should any woman commit suicide and it should always be out of love, not because of a ritual.

Suigan was repeating a ritualistic answer – just as the Shankaracharya of Puri is doing – without even understanding the meaning. The master was angry, because it was time that Suigan should understand the essential, existential experience that makes a man a buddha. That he was still a parrot made him angry.

So he asked, *"How can you escape birth and death?"*

A very essential point to be remembered: what words could not do, tears did. *Tears washed Suigan's face.* He could see the compassion of the master through the anger. And he could see that he himself was simply repeating the sutra. It was not his own understanding.

Tears washed Suigan's face as he bent his head.
After a few minutes he asked, "Please tell me
the summary of Buddhism."

He is now accepting: "I don't know, please tell me." And the master says the same thing. But something has changed in Suigan, that you have to understand. Tears have washed not only his face, but also his mind. Bending his head was a gesture saying, "I was pretending to be a knower, but I'm utterly ignorant. I am not even worthy of touching your feet." This acceptance of innocence and these tears create a totally new situation for the same sentence: *"If a cloud does not hang over the mountain, the moonlight will penetrate the waves of the lake."*

Before the teacher had finished speaking,
Suigan was enlightened.

Enlightenment is pure silence, the silence of no-mind. Your mind is continuously going on and on, yakkety-yak, yakkety-yak. Do you see it in the meditation? Do you think it is coming from somewhere outside? It is within you and you are hiding it. And my effort is to persuade you not to hide it, not to suppress it, to throw it out. Perhaps tears may come to your eyes or laughter and a deep understanding may arise.

If Suigan can become enlightened, why cannot you? It is everybody's birthright.

Before we try going into ourselves, into enlightenment, Maneesha has asked one question:

Beloved Bhagwan,
I have heard some sannyasins say, about fellow
sannyasins who decide to do something else
other than be here, "Oh well, perhaps they need
to do what they are doing." Is that true?

Maneesha, it is up to everyone. This place is not
a prison: you are here out of your own understanding. If you feel you need to be somewhere else,
don't wait a single moment, be where you feel to
be. I am all for freedom. Freedom is my religion.
Maneesha is asking:

On one hand I see that if we use everything we
decide to do, intelligently, of course we will
learn from it, so it can't be said we have missed,
or that we did not need to do it.

At least as far as I am concerned, everyone has to
decide for himself. I cannot force enlightenment on
you.
She is asking:

On the other hand, if we are going to decide
what we need to do, what is the point of being
with a master?

There is no point. The point is to be with *you!*
The master is non-essential. If you feel that being
with the master something is growing in you, that is
your decision. Otherwise, be anywhere you want,
but remember, you will not find another place on
earth at this moment to become enlightened. But

enlightenment is not a necessity for everyone: very few people can afford it because it is moving on a razor's edge. Certainly you cannot become enlightened intelligently. You can become enlightened only if your so-called intelligence is no longer interfering with your being.

What is your intelligence? Even the most intelligent people like Albert Einstein died without enlightenment. He left his brain to be examined, because he himself was wondering if there was something special in his brain that made him so intelligent. Perhaps, if it was known, it could be injected into everybody else. Maybe it was some protein, some vitamin, or some other chemical.

After his death his brain was examined thoroughly. It was the first time anybody's brain had been examined so thoroughly. He certainly had a few things more than ordinary people – some chemicals, twenty-six percent more. He was the most intelligent human being – yet, unenlightened. Intelligence has nothing to do with enlightenment.

Intelligence is part of your brain, your chemistry; and consciousness is not part of your chemistry: consciousness is your being, nobody can inject it. Enlightenment is simply becoming aware of your transcendence of chemistry and physics, biology and physiology, knowing yourself to be the eternal, non-physical energy. It is pure light, and nobody can enforce it, it is absolutely in your hands to remain ignorant or to become enlightened.

Before we try, a few laughs will be good to clean off the seriousness that has settled upon you.

Young Fagin Finkelstein, the advocate, is drafted to fight in Ronald Reagan's latest war with Iran. However, he manages to convince the draft-board officer that he is half-blind, and is sent home.

That evening Fagin goes to the movies, and at the end, when the lights come up, he notices that a member of the draft-board is sitting next to him.

Without a moment's hesitation, Fagin taps him on the arm and asks, "Excuse me, madam, but I wonder if you can help me. Is this the train for New Jersey?"

Sardar Gurudayal Singh is driving down M.G. Road one day in a brand new Maruti car. His friend, Sarjano, stops him and says, "Hey-a Sardarji, where did-a you get that brand-a new car?"

"Well," replies Sardar Gurudayal Singh, "I was going for a spin to Mulshi Lake on my old Yezdi motorbike, when I saw this sexy American girl, Ma Papaya Pineapple, stranded by the side of the road in this car. So I stopped and fixed the car for her."

"Far out-a," says Sarjano. "Then what happened?"

"Well," continues Sardar Gurudayal Singh, "Ma Papaya Pineapple looks at me in a very sexy way, nudges me in the belly and says, 'Thanks man, I'm really grateful. I will give you anything you want!'

"So naturally," adds Sardarji, "I took the Maruti!"

Three college boys go into their favorite coffee bar, only to find that their usual table is being occupied by an old woman. After debating what to do about the situation, they finally decide to embarrass the woman into leaving.

Sitting down next to the old lady, the first one says, "Hey guys, did you know that I was born three months before my parents were married?"

"That's nothing," says the next one. "I was born *six* months before my parents were married!"

"Guys," says the third, "my parents have *never* been married!"

The little old lady finally looks up from the table and says pleasantly, "Will one of you bastards pass the salt?"

Pope the Polack and Edwin Meese are arguing over what is considered man's greatest invention. Pope the Polack insists it is the wheel, "because that has made man mobile, and made it easier for me to spread the word of God."

But Meese claims it is the lever, "because that was the start of machinery, and machines have made us what we are today." They argue at length, but are unable to reach an agreement. Finally, Meese says, "Let us ask Ronald. He is the president – he knows *everything.*"

President Reagan tells them that they are both wrong. "Man's greatest invention is my thermos bottle," he declares.

"Your thermos bottle? You have got to be kidding!" says the Polack.

Reagan shakes his head and says, "It keeps my coffee warm in the winter and my juice cold in the summer."

"So?" queries Meese.

"Well," replies the president, "how does the thermos *know?*"

Now, the first drum, Rupesh, and everybody goes crazy; your best hit!

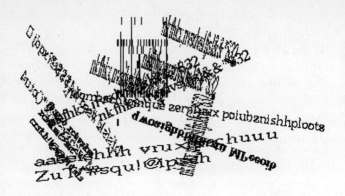

Rupesh…

Everybody becomes absolutely silent;
close your eyes;
go in.
No movement.
Deeper and deeper,
beyond the mind.
This is the message of all the buddhas:
just be.

Rupesh, beat the drum…

And everybody falls dead.

Let the body breathe; that is not your life.
Go deeper,
find out the life which needs no breathing.
It is just a pure space,
silent and joyous, a dance unto itself.
Drown in the dance.
This is the quantum leap,
from mind to no-mind.
So blissful is this evening,
so blessed are these moments.

Rupesh, beat the drum to bring everybody
back to life…

But come fresh, young, silent
and immensely alive.
Don't forget for a single moment this peace.
If it becomes your very life,
it is enlightenment.

Okay, Maneesha?
Yes, Bhagwan.
Are we allowed to celebrate?
YES!

THE BUDDHA
IS HIDING IN
THE PAPER BAG

Beloved Bhagwan,

*One day Ungan was ill and Dōgo asked him
a question: "When you are separated from your
bag-of-bones, where can I meet you again?"*

*Ungan replied, "Where there is no birth,
no dying."*

*Dōgo said, "Don't say that! Say, 'Where there is
not any no-birth and no-dying, and we don't
desire to meet each other again.' "*

*When Hofukū was about to die he said
to his monks, "For the last ten days my vitality
has decreased. It is nothing; simply the time
has come."*

*A monk said, "The time has come for you
to die – is that all right? To continue living
– is that all right?"*

Hofukū answered, "It is the way."

*The monk asked, "How can I stop
being flustered?"*

*Hofukū said, "It never rains but it pours." With
this, he sat in the zazen style and passed away.*

*Sōzan once said to Shie Doja, "Aren't you
'Paper Clothes the Pilgrim'?"*

Shie Doja answered, "I am not worthy of being so."

*Sōzan asked, "What is the thing beneath paper
clothes?"*

*Shie Doja said, "When just a leather garment is
put on the body, all things are of their suchness."*

*Sōzan said, "What is the activity beneath paper
clothes?"*

*Shie Doja came near him, did as he was asked,
and died standing up.*

*Sōzan said, "You have expounded the going,
but how about the coming?"*

*Shie Doja suddenly opened his eyes and asked,
"How about when a spiritual nature
does not borrow a placenta?"*

Sōzan said, "This is not yet wonderful."

Shie Doja asked, "What is wonderful then?"

Sōzan said, "Not-borrowing borrowing."

*Shie Doja thereupon said, "Be happy, be well!"
and died, sitting.*

Sōzan made a verse:

*The enlightened mind is a perfect
and formless body.
Do not believe, unreasonably,
That it is far off or near!
Thoughts of difference becloud
the original form.
A mind at variance with itself cannot be
in harmony with the way.
When emotion distinguishes phenomena,
we fall into materiality.
When intellect judges the manifold,
we lose the reality.
If you understand perfectly the meaning
of these words,
You are without doubt beyond danger
like those of ancient times.*

Maneesha, every master has shed tears for something very special that used to exist in the ancient
times. However, that very special thing is right now

here: the presence, the absolute silence; because only in this silence do you go beyond mind and beyond time. You enter into eternity.

This is what man has lost contact with. And to lose contact with eternity is to be like a tree uprooted from the earth. Man is also a tree. He also has roots, although they are invisible. And the contemporary mind has completely forgotten to water those roots, to keep the plant of consciousness alive, so that roses can blossom in your being.

I hope these anecdotes will take away all the nonsense that modern times have forced upon you and will give you a taste of eternity.

*One day Ungan was ill and Dōgo asked him
a question: "When you are separated from your
bag-of-bones, where can I meet you again?"
Ungan replied, "Where there is no birth,
 no dying."
Dōgo said, "Don't say that!"*

Now this is something to be understood. We ordinarily understand two things: the positive and the negative. Mind moves between the positive and the negative, for and against. Mind has no approach, no way to go beyond this polarity, this duality, this dialectic. And the whole experience of the buddhas emphasizes only this one thing, which is beyond duality and dialectics, beyond yes and beyond no. If you understand this transcendental experience, then this statement of Dōgo will be immediately understood.

Why did he say, "Don't say that"? Because Ungan has used the negative as an expression for the ultimate. That is not only Ungan's fallacy, it is the fallacy of the whole of humanity. Somebody believes in a positive god, in a positive philosophy; somebody negates the god, the heaven, the creation. But the

189

truth is neither Catholic nor Communist, neither in the yes nor in the no – but beyond both, in the silence.

When Ungan replied, "I am going where there is no birth, no dying," Dōgo was absolutely right to be angry with Ungan, when he said, *"Don't say that. Say, 'Where there is not any no-birth and no-dying, and we don't desire to meet each other again.'"*

Dōgo is very clear but only for those who have some experience of that which you cannot confine into the word 'life' or 'death', which you cannot confine into 'yes' or 'no', theism or atheism, which you simply say – through your silence, not through words. You indicate by your presence but not by language. If you try language, you are going to become entangled in difficulties.

Dōgo is trying to say that which cannot be said. 'Where there is not any no-birth' – now it is negation of negation. 'No-birth' is negation, and 'there is not any no-birth' is negation of negation. There have been philosophers whose whole philosophy is based on negating everything, negation included. Just deny everything and when nothing is left behind, that silence, that space is your authentic being.

And obviously he is right that, "We don't have any desire. So how we can have the desire of meeting each other again? We have met enough. I'm satisfied, you are satisfied, what is the point of meeting again? You are fulfilled, I'm fulfilled. Why bother about, why even enquire where we are going to meet?"

In other words he is saying: The moment you go beyond mind and time, you disperse in the whole. You don't exist as a separate entity. There is no question of meeting anybody. You have met with the whole in which everybody is included. The smallest pebble on the shore and the biggest star in the sky – both are meeting in that ultimate space. The sinner and the saint, the believer and the disbeliever, man or woman...it does not matter from what form you have come into the eternal. The moment you leave the form, you disappear into the formless. The question of meeting does not arise.

When Hofukū was about to die he said
to his monks, "For the last ten days my vitality
has decreased. It is nothing; simply the time
has come."
A monk said, "The time has come for you
to die – is that all right? To continue living
– is that all right?"
Hofukū answered, "It is the way."

Life comes, death comes; one is in one form, moves into another form and ultimately into the formless ocean of being – this is the way.

The monk asked, "How can I stop being
flustered?"
Hofukū said, "It never rains but it pours." With
this, he sat in the zazen style and passed away.

He sat silently in the lotus posture like Gautam Buddha, and passed away. Before passing away he said, *"It never rains but it pours."* You need not be flustered. You need not be worried. This is the way of things. One is born, one becomes young, one becomes old, one dies. There is nothing to be worried about. Everything in its time and everything is perfect. And when the moment comes, just sit down in silence and move into the formless.

Sōzan once said to Shie Doja, "Aren't you
'Paper Clothes the Pilgrim'?"

He used to use that name 'Paper Clothes Pilgrim'.

We are all paper clothes, covering something indefinable, indestructible.

Shie Doja answered, "I am not worthy of being so." "I have not yet discovered the one who is hiding behind the paper clothes; I am not worthy."

Sōzan asked, "What is the thing beneath paper clothes?"

"Why do you say you are not worthy? Just search a little bit behind the paper clothes." That's what we are doing every evening – searching behind the paper clothes, trying to find out what is hidden there.

Sōzan asked, "What is the thing beneath paper clothes?"

Shie Doja said, "When just a leather garment is put on the body, all things are of their suchness."

Sōzan said, "What is the activity behind paper clothes?"

He has not understood the answer that Doja has given. The moment you move behind your bodies which are nothing but paper clothes, what you find is pure suchness – *tathata,* thisness: a tremendously beautiful space but no entity as an ego, a space without boundaries, full of joy, full of peace, full of benediction.

But it is not a thing, you cannot hold it in your hand. It is not an object, it is your very subjectivity. It is your very innermost consciousness.

Shie Doja came near him, did as he was asked, – he was asked by Sōzan, *"What is the activity beneath paper clothes?"* He stood before Sōzan *and died standing up,* left the body, which remained simply a hollow bamboo without any music.

Sōzan said, "You have expounded the going," – certainly these people were strange people, worthy of the respect and dignity of all the centuries. Doja has died to show that which is hidden inside. He left the body, but Sōzan is not a lesser master than Doja.

Sōzan said, "You have expounded…"

Look, a dead body is standing before you and he is asking, *"You have expounded the going,* the death, *but how about the coming,* the birth?"

Perhaps there has never been such a conversation. A dead man is standing before you and you are asking a question. But this happens every day here when you all go into death…I go on talking to dead people. I say, "Die more deeply," because you only die just a little. You keep very close to the surface, so that if anything goes wrong, you can immediately come out. You just need Rupesh's drum and you are back. Die deeply, so that even if Rupesh drums on your head it will take a little time for you to come back.

Sōzan said, "You have expounded the going, but how about the coming?"

Shie Doja suddenly opened his eyes and asked, "How about when a spiritual nature does not borrow a placenta?"

These people are the very salt of the earth. Doja opened his eyes, came back into the body and said, *"How about when a spiritual nature does not borrow a placenta?"* – when a spiritual being does not enter into another womb to borrow a placenta?

Sōzan said, "This is not yet wonderful."

Shie Doja asked, "What is wonderful then?"

Sōzan said, "Not-borrowing borrowing."

Negation of negation. One borrows the placenta …the placenta is the connection between the mother and the child which is cut at the birth of the child. When one does not borrow a placenta…even the idea of not borrowing a placenta is enough to keep you away from the formless. You have to stop even not borrowing. Borrowing you have stopped, now stop not borrowing. You simply forget all about it, the negative and the positive, both. Don't look back, and disappear into the ocean.

Shie Doja thereupon said, "Be happy, be well!" and died, sitting.

Death seems to be a game to these people. It is a game: so is life. Don't take anything seriously. Life or death, both are just games and you are beyond both. You can participate on either side in the football match, but you are beyond the sides. For the moment you can play the game.

Sōzan on the death of Doja, *made a verse.* Such beautiful people! Somebody is dying and you make a verse.

*The enlightened mind is a perfect
and formless body.
Do not believe, unreasonably,
That it is far off or near!
Thoughts of difference becloud
the original form.
A mind at variance with itself cannot be
in harmony with the way.
When emotion distinguishes phenomena,
we fall into materiality.
When intellect judges the manifold,
we lose the reality.
If you understand perfectly the meaning
of these words,
You are without doubt beyond danger
like those of ancient times.*

This is my whole effort to introduce you to this same experience of the ancient buddhas, because it does not belong to time. It is a question of diving deep into yourself. The buddha is hiding in the paper bag. The paper bag may be of any shape: it may be male, it may be female; it may be young, it may be old; it may be black, it may be white…it does not mean anything to the inner consciousness. All distinctions are meaningless.

Your innermost being has always been perfect; it is just that you have completely forgotten to go into yourself. You go on and on, round and round the whole world, not knowing what you are searching for. Somebody is searching for power without knowing that power never satisfies anyone. Somebody is running after money, knowing perfectly well that there have been millions of people who have had an immense amount of money, and it does not help understanding. These are all unconscious ways of searching for something that you have already got within you. But the tendency of the mind is to look away, never to look to the obvious.

Meditation is to enter into the obvious. It is not even near, it is you. That's why Sōzan says, "It is neither far nor near." How can you be far or near? You are just here and you have been here always. Worlds have moved but you have gone nowhere, you cannot; wherever you go, you are there.

Meditation is simply a way to find the timeless, the eternal, your ultimate being. Without it, misery is your fate; without it, suffering is your lot; without it, you may have all the wealth of the world or all the power that any position can give you, but you will remain poor. There is only one thing that can make you an emperor and that is your own being. Just find it – it is hiding behind a paper bag.

It is not a great work: it is very simple. Just a little courage, a little risk of losing the paper bag. At the most, what can happen? When Rupesh gives the drumbeat to come back again, at the most you may not come. I don't think that is much trouble. We will still celebrate. So go deeply without any fear.

Before that, so you can die happily, a few laughs, because, one never knows, you may come back, you may not. Just for the journey, go laughing and dancing, if you are really going.

Young Dr. Dagburt goes out with Dr. Bones, a general practitioner, to observe him on home visits. "I will conduct the first two," says Bones. "Watch closely, then *you* give it a try."

At the first house, they are met by a distressed man. "My wife is having terrible stomach cramps," he says.

Dr. Bones does a brief examination, then gets on his hands and knees and looks under the bed. "Madam," says Bones, "you must cut out your ridiculous intake of sweets and chocolate, and you will be well in a day." Dagburt peeks under the bed and sees candy wrappers littering the floor.

On the next call they are met by a distraught Becky Goldberg. "It is Hymie, doctor!" she cries. "He was very forgetful all day yesterday, and today he has been falling over a lot. When I put him to bed, he passed out."

Examining Hymie, Bones gets down on the floor and looks under the bed. "It is a very simple problem," Bones says to Hymie. "You are drinking too much!" Young Dr. Dagburt sneaks a look under the bed and sees seven empty gin bottles.

At the third house, it is Dagburt's turn. He rings the doorbell and there is a long delay before a flushed young woman answers.

"Your husband asked us to call," says Dagburt. "He said you were not yourself this morning, and asked us to give you an examination."

So they go upstairs, and the woman lies down. Dagburt examines her and then he looks under the bed. "Okay," he concludes, "I prescribe you a dairy-free diet and you will be fine."

As they are leaving, Bones is puzzled and asks, "How did you reach that conclusion about the dairy-free diet?"

"Well," says Dagburt, "I followed your example and looked under the bed – where I found a milkman!"

Slobovia meets Kowalski at the "Pope and Hooker" pub for a few midnight beers.

"How is your wife's cooking?" asks Kowalski.

"I came home tonight," says Slobovia, "and my wife was crying and weeping because the dog had eaten a pie she made for me. 'Don't cry,' I told her, 'I will buy you another dog.'"

"Mr. Klopman," says Doctor Bones, "even though you are a very sick man, I think I will be able to pull you through."

"Doctor," cries Klopman, "if you do that, when I get well, I will donate five thousand dollars for your new hospital."

Months later, Bones meets Klopman in the street. "How do you feel?" he asks.

"Wonderful, doctor, just fine!" says Klopman. "Never felt better!"

"I have been meaning to speak to you," says Bones. "What about the money for the new hospital?"

"What are you talking about?" says Klopman.

"You said," replies Bones, "that if you got well, you would donate five thousand dollars for the new hospital."

"I said that?" asks Klopman. "That just shows how sick I was!"

Rupesh, give the first drum and everybody goes crazy.

Rupesh…

Everybody goes into deep silence.
No movement.
Become frozen just like stone statues.
Close your eyes; enter in.
Search behind the paper bags.
Deeper, deeper, deeper – without fear.
This is your own territory;
it belongs to no one except you.

In fact this is the only space
that belongs to you.
It is your eternity.

To take you deeper, Rupesh, give a beat and
everybody dies.

Die completely.
Don't be bothered about the paper bag.
This is the most beautiful graveyard.
So many consciousnesses reaching home,
touching their own depths.
This is what I have called
the quantum leap,
from mind to no-mind.
Rejoice in this silence,
let it penetrate to the very center of your being.
This is the greatest wonder in the world,
the most mysterious phenomenon.

Rupesh, bring the dead back to life.

This is resurrection.
Come back with a new insight and a new clarity,
a new silence and a new song,
a new dance in your being,
a new fresh breeze.

If this can become
your every moment experience,
underlying your whole life activity,
you have become a buddha.
To be a buddha is not a goal,
to be a buddha is the art of being alert,
aware, peaceful, loving.
Don't miss this moment
because nobody knows about the next.

Okay, Maneesha?
Yes, Bhagwan.
Can we celebrate because so many people are resurrected?
YES!

YOU CANNOT SEE
WITH YOUR EARS

Beloved Bhagwan,

Hyakujō needed to select a monk to be the master of a new monastery that was to be established on the mountain of Ta-Kuei-Shan.

He called the cook of his monastery and told him he had been chosen.

But the chief monk overheard Hyakujō's conversation with the cook and said, "No one can say that the cook monk is better than the chief monk."

So Hyakujō called all the monks together and told them the situation. He said that anyone who gave the correct answer to his question would be a candidate for the position in the new monastery.

Hyakujō then pointed to a water pitcher standing on the floor and said, "Without telling me its name, tell me what it is."

The chief monk said, "You cannot call it a wooden shoe."

When no one else answered, Hyakujō turned to the cook. The cook stepped forward, tipped over the pitcher with his foot and then left the room.

Hyakujō smiled and said, "The chief monk lost." The cook monk was made head of the monastery and lived there many years teaching more than one thousand monks in Zen.

In another incident, Kantaishi – a Confucian scholar – asked Daiten, who had a monastery in the place of exile, "How old are you?"

Daiten held out his rosary and said, "Do you understand?"

Kantaishi said, "No, I cannot understand."

Daiten replied, "In the daytime there are one hundred and eight beads and at night there are also one hundred and eight."

Kantaishi was very much displeased because he could not understand this old monk, and he returned home.

At home his wife asked, "What makes you so displeased?"

The scholar then told his wife all that had happened.

"Why not go back to the monastery and ask the old monk what he meant?" his wife suggested.

Next day, early in the morning, Kantaishi went to the monastery, where he met the chief monk at the gate.

"Why are you so early?" the chief monk asked.

"I wish to see your master and question him," Kantaishi answered.

"What is your business with him?" the chief monk asked. So the Confucian repeated his story.

"Why don't you ask me?" the chief monk inquired.

Kantaishi then asked, "What does 'one hundred and eight beads in the daytime and one hundred and eight beads at night' mean?"

The chief monk clicked his teeth three times.

At last Kantaishi met Daiten and once more asked his question, whereupon the master clicked his teeth three times.

"I know," said the Confucian, "all Buddhism is alike. A few moments ago I met the chief monk at the gate and asked him the same question and he answered me in the same way."

Daiten called the chief monk and said,

"I understand you showed him Buddhism a few minutes ago. Is it true?"

"Yes," answered the chief monk.

Daiten struck the chief monk and immediately expelled him from the monastery.

Maneesha, there are things which mind is naturally incapable of understanding. The mind has limitations, but our ego does not want to accept the limitations of the mind.

Every sense has its own limitation. You cannot see with your ears and you cannot hear with your eyes. In the same way, you can see objects with the mind but you cannot see the beyond, the formless with the mind. To the mind it will look absurd – just as to the blind man light is absurd and to the deaf, no music exists in the world. Those who have become too much identified with the mind and unfortunately all the civilizations and cultures that have existed in the world have enforced and reinforced the mind….

Zen is alone and unique. It points beyond the mind. So remember not to try to understand rationally, intelligently. Only in deep meditation and silence will you be able to feel the significance of these small anecdotes. They have something hidden in them, but it is not possible for the mind to figure it out. Put the mind aside, and suddenly you can see the truth which mind was blocking. As far as Zen is concerned, mind is a block to reality.

Except mind, nobody is hindering you declaring your buddhahood this very moment.

Hyakujō – a great Zen master – needed to select a monk to be the master of a new monastery that was to be established on the mountain of Ta-Kuei-Shan. He called the cook of his monastery and told him he had been chosen.

Before I proceed I have to say something about the cook, otherwise you will not be able to understand the whole story. This cook had entered the monastery as a young man thirty years before the incident when he was called by the master. Thirty years before when he had first entered, he had asked the master Hyakujō, "I don't know what I am searching for, I don't know the question; hence I cannot ask anything. If out of your compassion you can show me the way, I will be infinitely grateful." Hyakujō's monastery had one thousand monks, great scholars, intellectuals, philosophers. The poor man who had come said, "All that I can do is cook. I am uneducated."

The master said, "There is no problem. You start cooking. Just remember one thing: never come again to me. Whenever I need to, I will call you. Don't ask anyone anything; just remain like a shadow, working."

In China and Japan, rice is the main food. The cook was preparing rice for a thousand monks. He would get up early in the morning and go to bed late at night. There was no time for questioning, nor did he have any question. Just think: thirty years, cleaning rice, cooking rice. He became completely silent. He was not doing any meditation, but the mind was not needed. His work was so simple that mind retired on its own.

People had even forgotten that there was a monk

who never came to the assembly, who never asked anything, who never read any sutra. People had no idea even what his name was because he had never told anybody. Nobody had asked...even the master had not asked. This was the first time he had been called, when he was told he had been chosen to be the head of the new monastery that was being opened on a nearby mountain.

The master had been watching for thirty years. As the man became silent, his whole aura, his whole energy started showing the same light that surrounds a buddha. The master had been waiting for the right time. He called the cook and said, "You are to be the chief of the new monastery." Amongst one thousand scholars...choosing the cook, who knows nothing about Buddhism, who knows nothing about meditation, who knows nothing at all.

But the chief monk – Hyakujō's monastery of a thousand monks has one chief monk for day-to-day affairs – *overheard Hyakujō's conversation with the cook and said, "No one can say that the cook monk is better than the chief monk. I am the chief, and this is such stupidity that the cook should become the head of a great monastery on the mountain."*

So Hyakujō called all the monks together and told them the situation. He said that anyone who gave the correct answer to his question would be a candidate for the position in the new monastery.

Hyakujō then pointed to a water pitcher standing on the floor and said, "Without telling me its name, tell me what it is."

The chief monk said, "You cannot call it a wooden shoe."

This was not accepted. It said nothing about the water pitcher.

When no one else answered, Hyakujō turned to the cook. The cook stepped forward, tipped over the pitcher with his foot and then left the room.

Hyakujō smiled and said, "The chief monk lost."

The cook had said everything about the pitcher without uttering a single word. And he did not even wait to see whether he was chosen or not. Such unconcern for position, for power! Only such a man could be chosen to be the chief of a monastery where people are going to meditate.

The cook monk was made head of the monastery and lived there many years teaching more than one thousand monks in Zen.

It has been a wonder in the Zen tradition how the cook managed. He was absolutely uneducated. All that he had done his whole life was cook. Yet he managed to teach Zen to one thousand monks. The anecdote simply indicates that Zen is not an education, it is an experience. It is available to all: the uneducated, the educated, the young, the old, the brahmin, the sudra. It is available to all, if you can become silent.

The cook knew only how to be silent. He had become silent and he helped other people: "Just do the work you are doing the way I have been cooking for thirty years. Whatever you choose in the monastery do it with your totality. Here, there is no question, no answer – no scholarship. Just act with your totality – continuously – and wait for the right time."

The flower blossoms and the rain comes, the sun rises and the birds sing. Just like that – absolutely naturally – silence sprouts within you, brings flowers of the unknown, fills you with immense fulfillment. You know, although you cannot say a single word about it: you experience, but you have no explanation.

Life is a mystery that is the very essence of Zen.

Daiten replied in another incident when Kantaishi, a Confucian scholar...again I have to say something about Confucius. He is certainly nothing but confusion. His name absolutely gives the explanation about himself. He was a great scholar, perhaps the greatest that China has produced, and the most influential man in China's whole history.

He was a contemporary of Lao Tzu and had thousands of students. He was really a great intellect: he created the whole Chinese logic, and made all the social rules, ethos, morality. He controlled Chinese politics, and taught the kings and princes how to rule. He was a great man in every way. But his students many times told him, "A great desire arises in us. You should meet Lao Tzu."

Lao Tzu was unknown: a very small group of drop-outs followed him. He was such a strange fellow that no straightforward man was ever going to be close to him. He had his own way which eventually merged with Bodhidharma's.

Zen is the product of Bodhidharma and Lao Tzu: it is a crossbreed. Lao Tzu created great disciples like Chuang Tzu and Lieh Tzu but he could not create a religion, because he was against any organization; and he could not create scriptures because he was against saying something which cannot be said.

But still people felt, "That man has experienced something which we are missing. He is so content, with such grace, such beauty."

The disciples of Confucius told him, "He is by chance staying near here in a cave by the side of the river. It is a great chance for you both to meet. We would love to see what transpires."

It was below the ego of Confucius, but because again and again he was asked, he finally said, "Okay, I will come. I will see who this fellow is."

But he was also afraid. Every knowledgeable person is afraid, because basically he knows all his knowledge is borrowed. When an authentic person stands in front of him, the knower is absolutely naked, all his clothes drop off. He was afraid that Lao Tzu may be a dangerous experience, so he told his disciples to wait outside the cave. First he would go alone, get acquainted with Lao Tzu and then he would come out and take all the disciples in to meet Lao Tzu.

Within a few seconds he came out perspiring and told his disciples, "We are not going to see him again. And never ask me again. That man is danger-ous, very dangerous. He is not a man but a dragon. Never even touch his shadow."

What had transpired in that cave? What did Lao Tzu do to Confucius? The same as what happens when you encounter a lion. Lao Tzu was not a man of social conformity: he was not orthodox. He did not believe in any religion; he did not believe in any God; he did not believe in any morality.

He told Confucius, "You are confused and you are confusing others. First get totally conscious of your own being." That he calls *tao*. That is what Buddha calls *dhamma*. We can call it the truth, the ultimate truth. "First become acquainted with your inner nature and then talk about right and wrong and all that kind of nonsense. It is good that you have come because I was thinking one day to come and hit you on your head."

Confucius could not say a single word because it was all quite right: he had no idea who he was. Standing bare, naked before the disciples of Lao Tzu, he felt very much ashamed; he started perspiring. Lao Tzu shouted at him, "Get out if you cannot get in."

He escaped immediately to his disciples where he was a great man, a great scholar – even kings were his followers. He told his disciples, "Never, never come across this fellow. He will destroy you. He will take away your personality. He will leave you utterly innocent when education is needed, culture is needed, civilization is needed. That man is absolutely against any education, any civilization, any culture. He wants only freedom and spiritual growth."

This incident happened between Kantaishi, a Confucian scholar, and Daiten, a Zen master.

Kantaishi asked the Zen master, "How old are you?"

There was a period of silence. Daiten looked into the eyes of the Confucian scholar, held out his rosary and said, *"Do you understand?"*

Kantaishi said, "No, I cannot understand."

Daiten replied, "In the daytime there are one hundred and eight beads and at night there are also one hundred and eight."

Kantaishi was very much displeased because he could not understand this old monk, and he returned home.

At home his wife asked, "What makes you so displeased?"

The scholar then told his wife all that has happened.

"Why not go back to the monastery and ask the old monk what he meant?" his wife suggested.

Next day, early in the morning, Kantaishi went to the monastery, where he met the chief monk at the gate.

"Why are you so early?" the chief monk asked.

"I wish to see your master and question him," Kantaishi answered.

"What is your business with him?" the chief monk asked. So the Confucian repeated his story.

"Why don't you ask me?" the chief monk inquired.

Kantaishi then said, "What does 'one hundred and eight beads in the daytime and one hundred and eight beads at night time' mean?" The chief monk clicked his teeth three times.

At last Kantaishi met Daiten and once more asked his question, whereupon the master clicked his teeth three times.

"I know," said the Confucian, "all Buddhism is alike. A few moments ago I met the chief monk at the gate and asked him the same question and he answered me in the same way."

Daiten called the chief monk and said, "I understand you showed him Buddhism a few minutes ago. Is it true?"

"Yes," answered the chief monk.

Daiten struck the chief monk and immediately expelled him from the monastery.

This has been asked again and again in the history of Zen. What transpired? First, the master is telling the disciple to be the same in the day and in the night, to be the same in suffering and in rejoicing, the same when young or when old, to be the same when alive and when dead. That was the meaning of showing the rosary which remains the same whether it is day or night.

The puzzle is that the chief monk of the monastery answered in the same way. When the Confucian scholar came the second time, the chief monk was at the gate. He clicked his teeth three times. The Confucian scholar was even more confused. The first time he had come to ask, "What does it mean by showing a rosary and saying that it remains the same in the night and in the day?" And now this chief monk has given him another problem. He clicked his teeth three times.

But he did not take this answer, he wanted to ask the master himself. The master also clicked his teeth three times. Clicking the teeth three times is a symbol in Zen meaning, "You can go on asking, but it does not help. One mystery will be answered by another mystery." Clicking three times gives you a chance to put the mind aside and just listen to the clicking of the teeth.

The master is saying, "All philosophy, all questions, all answers are nothing but the clicking of teeth. Stop all this nonsense." But the scholar said, "That means that Buddhism is the same." He cannot put his mind aside. Where is Buddhism in this? The rosary is not Buddhist, nor is being the same in the day and the night. And what is Buddhist in clicking your teeth? But because the chief monk has also clicked his teeth, his mind, the scholarly mind, concludes, "It seems both these people are saying that Buddhism is the same everywhere."

When he said, *"I know all Buddhism is alike. A few moments ago I met the chief monk at the gate and asked him the question and he answered me in the same way."*
Daiten called the chief monk and said,
"I understand you showed him Buddhism a few minutes ago? Is it true?"
"Yes," answered the chief.
Daiten struck the chief monk and immediately expelled him from the monastery.

The question has been asked why the chief monk was expelled from the monastery. His education is complete. Zen has its own way of certifying; he has graduated. You can never take Zen for granted.

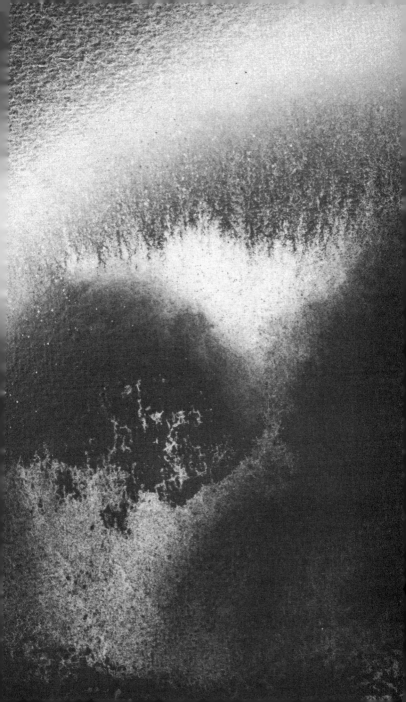

Every Zen master has his own way and that was his way of telling him, "Now there is no need to be here. Get out! You have graduated. Now you know. So why waste time? Give the place to somebody else, some other unwise person, some other seeker, and you go and spread what you have understood."

This expulsion is not ordinary expulsion. This expulsion is a certificate. Zen is so strange in its way; when it wants to appreciate it hits, it beats. But its whole effort is to open you up to the unknown no-mind. Once you experience the silence of your being, there is nothing more to be learned, nothing more to be gained, nothing more to be known, nowhere to go. There is just a laugh that you have been such an idiot, searching for yourself when you have been always in, while you were searching all over the world.

Maneesha's question is:

Beloved Bhagwan,
It really seems that for the first time those of us who are with you are not setting up any kind of spiritual or organizational hierarchy: there is just you and us – and even that division disappears in the silence here each evening.

Maneesha, I have not been here for thirty-five years. And in this absence of thirty-five years I have been trying to help everybody be as absent as I am. In this absence, I have known the greatest ecstasy and I have known life in its pure essence without any reason or rhyme, just as flowers blossom and spread their fragrance. There is no effort in it. Without any effort I have been sharing myself to anyone who by chance has come across me.

I am not, and I want you also to be not. The more

you are, the more you will suffer. The more you are, the more you are in hell. If you want to be more, go to Europe and do Fischer-Hoffman therapy. That leads you directly to hell. Its whole effort is to make you more, stronger, to give you a personality.

Here, my whole work is anti Fischer-Hoffman. I want you to be nobody, nothing, just a silence; because only in this silence have buddhas blossomed. Every day you have some feel of it. One day, suddenly, this feel will become your very breathing, the very beating of your heart. I declare this assembly to be the most blessed on the earth at this moment. Everywhere, there is the clicking of teeth. This small assembly of seekers is moving in a totally different dimension to the mind. It is moving in the dimension of no thought, no feeling, no emotion – just pure nothingness.

Once you have attained to pure nothingness you have found the dance of the universal, of the eternal. You have found the meaning of life. There is no other way to find the significance and the fragrance of your own being.

Before we enter into our silence, into the very essence of Zen, the bamboos are silent, waiting for a few laughs from you. Shunyo informed me yesterday that, since these meditations, since this silence and this laughter have begun, the bamboos have grown so much and new sprouts have come.

Just for these bamboos, particularly for the new ones...

The famous Indian driver, Rambo Rickshaw, is chewing pan and hanging out at the Kit-Kat Restaurant. Suddenly, Swami Herschel comes running up. "Quick!" says Herschel, "I am sick! Do you know where Ruby Hall is?"

"How are you?" says Rambo Rickshaw. "What is your country?"

"Please, I'm very ill," pleads Herschel. "Do you know Ruby Hall?"

"Where you are going? England? Are you England-man?" asks Rambo.

"Help," moans Herschel, turning a little green "…Ruby Hall."

"Airport going? No problem!" says Rambo.

"Quickly," gasps Herschel, lying in the back seat. "Can you take me to…"

"Where you are going?" says Rambo. "Germany? Are you Germany-man?"

"Aaahhg!" groans Herschel.

"M.G. Road? Shopping? Change money?" asks Rambo Rickshaw.

"No, no, Ruby Hall, Ruby Hall!" gasps Herschel.

"Ruby Hall? That is hospital. You are sick?" says Rambo.

"Jesus Christ!" yells Herschel.

"Oh, you are American," smiles Rambo. "I know California. You want Poona tour?"

"No!" cries Herschel, "I want fucking Ruby Hall!"

"Fucking who?" shouts Rambo Rickshaw. "No! Get out! No fucking here!"

One Saturday night George ends up at a party in an unfamiliar apartment building. He gets very drunk, but somehow finds his way home in the small hours of the morning. He wakes up the next afternoon with a terrible hangover, and he realizes that he has left his jacket, tie, shirt and shoes at the party.

With much difficulty he finds the apartment building, but has no idea which apartment he had been in. The only thing he remembers is that it had a magnificent gold toilet. So he knocks at the first apartment.

The door is answered by a man with a hangover.

"Hello," says George, "did you have a party here last night?"

"We sure did," groans the man.

"And do you have a gold toilet?" asks George.

"A gold toilet? We sure don't!" replies the man.

This happens in almost every apartment. Everyone is recovering from a party, but no one knows anything about a gold toilet.

At the last apartment, the door is opened by a man with a hangover. "Hello," says George, "did you have a party last night?"

"Boy! We sure did," groans the man.

"And do you have a gold toilet?" asks George.

There is a long silence. Finally, the man shouts back into the apartment, "Hey, Harry! Here is the guy who shit in your tuba!"

God is speaking to Moses on the mountain, and Moses is shaking his head in disbelief.

With his face upturned towards heaven, Moses says, "Now let me get this straight, God. You are telling me that *we* are the chosen people, and so you want us to cut off the tips of our *what?*"

Now, let God figure it out. Obviously, he cannot use a dirty word. He is in the same difficulty as Zen. He knows what it is but he cannot say it.

Rupesh, the first drum and everybody goes crazy.

Rupesh…

Everyone becomes silent.
Close your eyes, no movement.
Just go in.
Deeper and deeper.
You don't have to lose anything.
You can only find yourself.
This is the way
that leads to your ultimate destiny.
This is the quantum leap
from mind to no-mind.
Just be.

Rupesh…

Everyone dies.
Die completely.
Body continues breathing – no harm.
You just go in.
At the most, you may not return.
But don't hesitate
because ahead of you is eternity.
Just a moment, a jump from the mortal
into the immortal.

Rupesh…

Come back to life, resurrected, new.
Let the past die
so that you can be unburdened, light,
and you can have wings to fly.

Okay, Maneesha?
Yes, Bhagwan.
Can we celebrate for those who have resurrected?
YES!

MIND WITH
A SMALL m

Beloved Bhagwan,

*A non-Buddhist presented Hōgen with a screen
that had a picture painted on it. When he had
finished looking at it, Hōgen said, "Did you
paint this with your hand or your mind?"*

The artist answered, "With my mind."

Hōgen said, "What is this mind of yours?"

The artist had no answer.

Maneesha, before I discuss the Zen anecdote I
have to say a few things to my sannyasins here or
anywhere else in the world.

Write to the Nobel Prize committee that this old
goat, the Shankaracharya of Puri, needs a Nobel
Prize. And be quick, otherwise he will commit suicide, though that would not matter, even if the
Nobel Prize had to be given posthumously. I have
talked about the Shankaracharya, who continuously insists that *sati pratha* should be legalized
and incorporated in the constitution of India.

Now he has come with a great original idea. For
this original idea he needs, deserves a Nobel Prize.
In Hyderabad there are no rains this year. He has
said that if a woman commits sati, hara-kiri, rains
would come. In the whole history of Hinduism
there is not a single scripture describing any connection between a woman committing suicide,
being burned alive, and the rains coming. For
what? To quench the fire of the funeral?

But it is strange that in a country which is now
bulging with a population of almost one billion,
nobody opposes such stupid ideas. It seems
nobody is concerned with what happens to man

and his future. These priests have exploited man for centuries, have destroyed his dignity. They have been the greatest slave-makers. Half of society consists of women and they have taken all freedom from them, even the freedom to breathe. They want women to commit suicide.

This person should be immediately imprisoned. He has to prove on what grounds, for what reason a woman burning alive can bring clouds? And as I have said, he should commit suicide himself to prove it; that would be more manly and more courageous.

Secondly, just like the women, in this country a great number of people have suffered for centuries; they have been called untouchables. If even their shadow touches you, you have to take a bath. Such insult, such humiliation!

A new temple is raised, where the untouchables, to whom Gandhi gave that name *'harijans',* meaning God's men...clever politics, cunning diplomacy. If these are God's men, what is everybody else? And these "God's men" have been suffering for centuries: they are not permitted to read any Hindu scripture or enter any Hindu temple.

And because harijans are trying to enter this temple, suddenly all the Hindu chauvinists, who would not have dared to say anything against the Shankaracharya, are now demanding that he should retire from his post, because he is preventing the harijans from entering the temple.

Man's history is full of strange turns. On this point all Hindu scriptures are in favour of the Shankaracharya. If the politicians want to allow harijans into Hindu temples, they should burn all Hindu scriptures. But everybody's concern is votes. Nobody is concerned with the untouchables, the harijans, or their entry into the temple; the question is, "Should they remain part of Hindu society?" Their number is twenty-five crore, one fourth of Hindu society. Even a man like Mahatma Gandhi was against giving harijans a separate vote, though it could give them a certain independence from centuries of slavery.

My own suggestion is that in the first place no harijans should enter any Hindu temple. They should avoid Hindu temples, scriptures, these so-called Shankaracharyas, and should simply declare themselves independent of Hindus. They are enough, twenty-five crore; they can rule over the country! But political parties want them to remain Hindus, because of their voting strength. The politicians are willing even to condemn the Shankaracharya who is right as far as Hindu tradition is concerned. He is perfectly right, because for five thousand years no harijan has ever entered any Hindu temple.

But they are suddenly against the Shankaracharya, because he is creating trouble. If these harijans separate themselves from the Hindu fold, the whole destiny of the nation will be different. But they are poor, uneducated, because they have not been allowed any education; they have not been allowed any job other than the ones they have been doing traditionally, the lowest jobs: cleaning people's toilets, making shoes, butchering animals. They have not been able to move into any other work.

But even Mahatma Gandhi was afraid – and I don't know why people go on calling him Mahatma. The word means 'the great soul', but the soul was not very great, it was absolutely political, diplomatic. He fasted for twenty-one days against harijans getting a separate vote. The separate vote was only a symbol that was going to create for hari-jans a strength of their own. But they don't have to become anything, they don't have to become Christians, they don't have to become Mohammed-ans, they don't have to become Buddhists; nobody needs religion, everybody needs individuality, awareness.

And this is a good chance for harijans, but such is foolishness...although for centuries they have been pushed back from the temples and burned alive if found reading the scriptures, they still go on cling-ing and asking to enter into Hindu temples. There is no need for anybody to enter any temple, any synagogue, any church, any mosque. This whole universe is your temple and your being is the only scripture you have to read.

I am saying this, because Hindu chauvinists are trying to force harijans to enter the temples, while more orthodox Hindus are trying to prevent them. The whole thing is so stupid! The harijans should simply refuse to enter any Hindu temple or any Mohammedan mosque or any church. You are enough unto yourself. If I don't need any religion, if I don't need any temple, if I don't need any scripture, if I'm sufficient unto myself, why cannot *you* be?

But it seems the slaves are as much responsible for slavery as the slave-makers themselves. The slaves want to be slaves: they want to be depen-dent. They are afraid, without the priesthood, with-out the temples, of what would happen to their spiritual growth. I say to everyone: spiritual growth is an individual affair, it needs no organization, it needs no special place, it needs only for you to enter into your own space.

A non-Buddhist presented Hōgen with a screen that had a picture painted on it. When he had

*finished looking at it, Hōgen said, "Did you
paint this with your hand or your mind?"*

I have to remind you of one thing: Buddhists
write 'mind' with a small m, when they mean 'your
mind'. And when they want to mean 'the universal
mind', they write 'mind' with a capital M.

In this question Hōgen has asked about a small-m
mind.

The artist answered, "With my mind," – small m.
Hōgen said, "What is this mind of yours?"
The artist had no answer.

Poor artist! A very ordinary artist, who knows
nothing of the intricacies and the workings of the
mind – what to say about the no-mind? – facing a
great master. And if a picture comes from your
mind, it is going to be just a reflection of your craziness, insanity. Unless you know the no-mind,
unless you know the space beyond mind, your
painting, your poetry, your music cannot be sane.

We are living on an insane planet. From the
second world war to today, without any great war
happening, seventeen million people have been
killed in small wars, which people hardly notice. Is
something basically wrong with the mind? It is vio-
lent, murderous, suicidal, it gives you misery, suffering, agony, anguish, and still you go on clinging to it.

This has to be remembered by my people, that
unless your art, your creation comes out of your
meditation, it has no value at all. Out of meditation,
out of silence, every song becomes Solomon's
song, and every picture represents, as a mirror will
represent, a buddha. Before you create anything,
uncreate your mind.

The artist was really very poor. I want you to be
really rich, and there is only one richness which is
hidden deep, very deep inside you. It is beyond the

reach of your thought, of your reason, it is available only to those who can be utterly silent. Once you have got it, the very kingdom of God is yours. Then whatever comes out of it has a beauty, a blissfulness, an ecstasy.

Bashō wrote:

The beginning of all art:
a song when planting a rice-field
in the country's inmost part.

It does not matter what you are doing; what matters is: is the inner space silent? Then even planting seeds in a field, you yourself become a song, you yourself become a dance.

Bashō also wrote:

"...All who have achieved real excellence in any
art, possess one thing in common, that is, a
mind to obey nature, to be one with nature,
throughout the four seasons of the year.
Whatever such a mind sees is a flower, and
whatever such a mind dreams of is the moon. It
is only a barbarous mind that sees other than
the flower, merely an animal mind that dreams
of other than the moon."

Our so-called mind is almost four million years old. It has passed through very dark nights, when there was no fire, no clothes, no houses; it has lived for millions of years in constant danger. That has made it aggressive, afraid, defensive, always being afraid of the dark night, of the wild animals. The mind carries those four million years of darkness, the fear of death. Hence it is afraid, although the situation has changed. Now there are no wild animals except you. But the mind knows nothing of the present, it carries only the past.

If you want to know the universe and its mystery, you have to take a jump out of the mind.

Shataku wrote:

Mind set free in the Dharma-realm,
I sit at the moon-filled window
Watching the mountains with my ears,
Hearing the stream with my open eyes.
Each molecule preaches perfect law,
Each moment chants true sutra:
The most fleeting thought is timeless.
A single hair is enough to stir the sea.

And Gotsuan wrote:

With no-mind I have enjoyed my stay,
With mind I return to So, my homeland.
Whether in mind or not,
I am content en route to heaven.

These people are talking about things which cannot be said, but out of compassion they are trying to make all kinds of effort to indicate to you your very being, which is your freedom; otherwise, everybody is a prisoner.

When I was imprisoned in America, the sheriff of the jail fell in love with me. He said to me, "Do you feel humiliated, because your hands are cuffed, your feet have chains, your waist has chains, do you feel humiliated?"

I said, "Everybody is a prisoner, just these handcuffs and these chains don't make any difference. You are also a prisoner but your chains are invisible."

He was a little puzzled, an old man, but very intelligent. He said, "I don't understand."

I said, "You will have to meditate to see the point that your body is your prison, your mind is nothing but your chains. And I am not humiliated; these handcuffs and these chains that you have put on me simply expose everyone else's reality. As far as I am concerned, I am free. No chain, no handcuffs, no prison cell can hold me. I can move out, open my wings and be in the eternal – it does not matter."

He was very respectful. He used to come to see me about six times a day and he asked me, "What are you doing all the time? I am the sheriff of seven hundred prisoners here, but you are the strangest, you simply go on sitting."

I said, "It is such a rare opportunity not to move, not to do anything, not to have to remember if it is seven o'clock when I go to my people. I have never been so free."

He said, "You are strange, but the whole staff has fallen in love with you."

The moment I left that jail he said, "I know you have to go from here, but deep down none of my staff nor the prisoners want you to leave. Why can't you stay here? In three days the whole climate of my jail has changed."

I said, "I would love to be here, but my people are waiting. Next time, when I decide to have another taste, I will come directly to North Carolina in America."

He said, "You are always welcome, whether you are arrested or not, whether any court wants you to be in the jail or not. As far as I'm concerned, my doors are open."

There is only one freedom, the freedom to be; there is only one life, that which is hidden within you. The moment you touch it, you have moved beyond words, you have heard the celestial song and a dance that continues from eternity to eternity.

Maneesha has asked:

Beloved Bhagwan,
It feels to me as if this discourse series has been
more like a class in sculpting or painting, be-
cause you have invited us to help create each
evening – to weave the silk of silence, to dance
with death and awake again, each of us, a
Master-piece.

Maneesha, your question is not a question, but only a statement of the truth.

Before we enter this moment, I think a cup of coffee would not be... Sardarji sounds very happy. This time he is sitting nearby. Basically he belongs where the bamboos are, just a turbanned bamboo.

Ronald Reagan takes Margaret Thatcher and Pope the Polack out to lunch. They go to President Reagan's favorite family restaurant, the 'Buns and Breasts Chicken House.'

After drinking a little too much wine with lunch, the slightly tipsy trio orders coffee. As it is being served, Ronald Reagan leans over to Margaret Thatcher's ear. With a devilish grin he slurs, "In America we say 'Pass the honey, honey.'"

The prime minister smiles and bats her eyelashes. Then stroking Pope the Polack's fingers sensuously, she slurs, "In England we say 'Pass the sugar, sugar.'" Then she says, "What do you say where you come from, Pope-sy wope-sy?"

Pope the Polack smiles and, straightening his collar, gives Margaret his best Valentino eyes. Then in a low voice he says, "Pass the tea...bag."

The phone rings at the Camp David motorpool and Private Leroy Jackson answers it.

"Where is that limousine that was ordered half an hour ago?" screams a voice at the other end. "Why is it taking so long?"

"Oh, you mean the limo for old Colonel Fat-Ass!" replies Leroy.

"What did you say?" cries the other voice.

"Er...who is this calling?" says Leroy, sheepishly.

"You don't know? This is Colonel Hawkbutt! And who are you?" demands the Colonel.

"You don't know?" says Leroy. "Well then – bye, bye, Fat-Ass!"

The Bishop of Mississippi and his wife are owners of a magnificent parrot. But the parrot is a great embarrassment to the bishop because of its very unreligious language. However, his wife is devoted to the bird and will not get rid of it because of its great intelligence.

One day they are playing host to a new black preacher visiting from Chicago. The local people are not happy about having a black man preach in their church, but the bishop is doing everything he can to be polite.

After the services, the bishop and his wife are having coffee and a snack with the preacher in their home.

The black man sees the parrot in the corner and is impressed by its beautiful feathers.

"Say something to him," urges the bishop's wife. "And he will give you a reply."

So the preacher walks over with a little piece of food and says, "Polly wanna cracker?"

The parrot eyes the black man suspiciously, and then shrieks, "Nigger wanna watermelon?"

Now, Rupesh, give the first beat of the drum and everybody goes absolutely crazy…

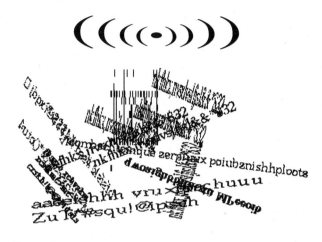

Rupesh…

Be silent. Close your eyes. No movement.
Just be in.
This is *it,* your very being, your eternity,
your freedom from all limitations.
This silent space is what makes you a buddha.
In this moment
I am surrounded by thousands of buddhas.
To be a buddha is your birthright.
That is the quantum leap,
from mind to no-mind.
Mind makes you just an old ancient animal.
And no-mind brings a new universe
of ecstasy and blessings;
thousands of roses blossom in this space.

Now to make it deeper, Rupesh give the drum
a good beat and everybody dies...

Die totally.
Let the body breathe, don't bother,
you just go on digging deeper and deeper
within yourself.
There somewhere is the door
of the kingdom of God, so close
that it is unbelievable how one can forget it.
Once you have a taste of it,
keep it whatever you do,
just as an undercurrent.
Let this silence remain dancing.

Rupesh...

Come back to life. Be a sitting buddha,
but keep the touch and the connection.
Never for a single moment
forget your divineness.

Okay, Maneesha?
Yes, Bhagwan.
Can we celebrate the resurrection of so many
buddhas?
YES!

CAN WE
CELEBRATE NOW?

Beloved Bhagwan,

Haikyu said, "Illusion obstructs the Mind; how can illusion be got rid of?"

Obaku said, "Creating illusion, getting rid of illusion – both these are illusion, for illusion has no root; it appears by reason of discrimination. If you do not think of contraries, such as ordinary and superior, illusion ceases of itself, and how can you then get rid of it? When there is not a hair's breadth of something to rely on, this is called 'Giving away with both hands, and thus receiving buddhahood.'"

Haikyu said, "There being nothing to rely on, how can anything be transmitted?"

Obaku said, "Mind is transmitted by Mind."

Haikyu said, "If the Mind is transmitted, why do you say there is no such thing as Mind?"

Obaku said, "Not receiving the law is called 'transmission of Mind'. If you understand what this Mind is, this is the No-Mind, the No-Law."

Haikyu said, "If there's no Mind, and no Law, how can you talk about 'transmitting' something?"

Obaku said, "When you hear me say 'transmission of Mind,' you think of there being a 'something' to transmit, so a patriarch declared:

'When you realize the nature of Mind, You speak of it as a wonderful mystery; Enlightenment is unattainable. When attained, you do not describe it as something known.'

Obaku said, "If I get you to understand this, do you think you could?"

Maneesha, before I discuss the last sutra of this series, I have to say something about the British Parliament.

After two years the British Parliament is still discussing me, and the Home Minister lied just like any politician. He said I was not allowed entry, because I could have destroyed the morality, the religion, the character of the country.

In the first place I never asked for entry into England. How can you deny a man entry who has not asked for it? I had asked only to stay for six hours in the night in the international airport lounge, because my pilot's time for running the jet was finished. He had to take a rest by law.

From the lounge, in the middle of the night, within six hours, how could I manage to destroy the British character, morality, religion? I had no idea – otherwise I would not have asked about staying even though it was my right – that the British morality, character, religion all live in the lounge of the international airport.

I had not asked for any entry and I will never ask, because Britain is the most barbarous country of this century. They have oppressed almost half the world, raped, murdered, and still they think they have morality, religion, culture. Even if this Home Minister requests me, I am not going to spit on his face in the British Parliament.

I want him to answer to the British Parliament, because he has been deceiving his own country by stating a lie.

But the whole business of politicians is lying.

Just today I have received the information that

one Arya Samaj leader, Swami Agnivesh, wants untouchables allowed into Hindu temples. It is strange and apparently contradictory, but not really so. The Shankaracharya of Puri is insisting that no harijan can enter a Hindu temple and another Hindu leader is trying to let them in. It appears a contradiction, but it is not; both are playing politics.

Swami Agnivesh wants them to enter temples not because he's against the Hindu scriptures and against the whole Hindu tradition, but just because harijans have twenty-five crore votes. They are poor people, oppressed for centuries and not allowed any education, but it needs no education to see that if a religion does not want you to enter its temples or to read its scriptures, then it's not worth being a part of it.

Every harijan should get out of the Hindu fold. That will mean they will have one fourth of the parliament in their hands. For the first time in history let the oppressed, the enslaved be the rulers. And women, whether they are harijan or not, should support harijans, because they have been treated in the same way by the Hindus.

But it seems man's mind is so irrational that women are the only people who go to the temples and these same temples have reduced women to a secondary status. Hindu *shastras* say that women should be treated just like animals, and still women go on worshipping these *shastras* and going to these temples.

Thousands of harijans have been burned alive down the ages. Even today, whole villages are burned, their animals, their children, their old people...everybody is burned except young women who are raped. Still they want to go to the temples of these same people! They have to remind themselves that these Hindus are human beings!

Religion has nothing to do with temples. Religion is something about finding yourself, about knowing your eternal consciousness; it does not need any priest as a mediator between you and existence. But the priesthood all over the world has been insisting that religion is their monopoly. You cannot have a direct, intimate love affair with existence; it has to be "care of" the priest, the pope.

Just a few months ago the pope created a sin, which has never existed before. The new sin is to confess directly to God. You have to confess to the priest who will take care of you, because he has a direct line to God.

The world is tortured by two kinds of people, the politicians and the priests. Both are liars. The priest does not know truth, because it is not written in the scriptures, and politicians are just beggars, suffering from an inferiority complex. They are trying to be powerful by begging votes to convince themselves that they are not inferior, but are superior beings.

Do you hear all the birds giving their support?

Unfortunately even the birds are freer than you. All your religions are your imprisonment, they are your chains. If you really want to taste existence and its dance, then you have to renounce not the world, but religions and their scriptures, you have to renounce the priests, the temples, the synagogues, you have to come directly in contact with your being, because there is the door to the kingdom of God. Everyone individually is capable of rejoicing in this beautiful existence, in the divinity of everything that is. No temples are needed, no statues are needed, no scriptures are needed; what is needed is a deep silence and a search within yourself.

I would like to say to the harijans of this country,

"Please, get out of the Hindu fold." Nor should women support Hinduism, because Hinduism has been murdering thousands of women in the name of *sati pratha*. This is the ugliest thing that anybody can do, forcing millions of women down the centuries to be burned alive on their husbands' funeral pyre. This is not religiousness, this is simply male-chauvinistic bondage of women, of the poor, of the oppressed.

We have been waiting for three hundred years to get rid of the British Empire. They exploited this country to the point where the Prime Minister, Attlee, under whom India became independent, sent Mountbatten as Governor-General of India with a message to make the country free quickly; otherwise, "...all its poverty, all its exploding population, all its starving millions will be our burden." Attlee insisted on speed, giving an exact date by which they should move out.

They sucked the blood of the country and their Home Minister thinks they are a religious people. They murdered and corrupted almost half of humanity without any concern for life; and I cannot stay in their airport for six hours when they stayed in this country for three hundred years. What right did they have?

And the same applies to the brahmins. What right do they have that they should prevent the oppressed of centuries from even entering the temples? What harm can they do?

But the whole history of religion is just a history of bloodshed. A better humanity will be without organized religions; a better humanity will respect the individual, will not take away the dignity of anyone, man or woman, black or white. Religiousness concerns itself with freedom, with consciousness, with exploring the divine which is spread all over the place, in the trees and in the stars, in the birds, in the rivers and in the mountains. There is one soul: we are part of it.

Nobody is born a Hindu or a Mohammedan, a Christian or a Communist; everybody is born as an innocence. To regain that innocence is my whole effort here. I call this place really holy and sacred. All other temples are only so-called; they are profane, because they have been committing all kinds of crime against the growth of humanity, its spirituality, its love, its intelligence.

These sutras are concerned with authentic religion, they are concerned with *you,* in your deepest consciousness, in your flowering as individual roses.

Haikyu said, "Illusion obstructs the Mind; how can illusion be got rid of?"

The question seems to be relevant and logical because all the buddhas, all the awakened ones have said that illusion obstructs the Mind. Mind with a capital "M" means consciousness; it is not your small mind but the mind of the whole of existence.

English is a poor language compared to Sanskrit, particularly as far as religious experience is concerned. Sanskrit has a dozen names for different qualities of consciousness, just as Eskimos have twelve names for ice. No other language needs that many: Eskimos know the different qualities, because they have lived for centuries in the snow. And in this country many people have blossomed to the moment where they are no longer bodies and no longer with a small mind, but have become the very mind of the universe.

The question Haikyu is asking is relevant: *"Illusion obstructs..."* so say all the buddhas: *"how can illusion be got rid of?"* Obviously, he is asking for a method, a technique. And that is where people get lost. You cannot get rid of illusions. Can you get rid of your dreams? When you are dreaming you cannot get out of it and get back into it.

One night, Mulla Nasruddin nudged his wife in the middle of the night, "Bring my glasses, quick."

The wife said, "What is the matter? What are you going to do in the night with glasses?"

He said, "Don't argue. Argue in the day. Now just bring the glasses. I was seeing such a beautiful woman and you know my eyesight is not good."

He put on his glasses and tried hard to find the woman. He could not find her, but only found his wife laughing, "You are an idiot. Even in your sleep you are an idiot."

You cannot throw a dream away, you cannot create it, you cannot uncreate it, but you can still get out of it by becoming aware, by simply jumping out of bed.

Obaku said to Haikyu's question, *"Creating illusion, getting rid of illusion – both these are illusion, for illusion has no root; it appears by reason of discrimination. If you do not think of contraries, such as ordinary and superior,* the sudra and the brahmin, the black and the white, *illusion ceases of itself, and how can you then get rid of it* when it has ceased? Do you ask when you wake up how to get rid of the dreams?"

Once you are awake you never ask. Not a single person in the whole of history has ever asked; when he is awake he is out of the dreams and there is no question of getting rid of them. The very idea of "getting rid of" means you still have it. This is a very significant statement by Obaku that, "Illusion

247

is illusion. Getting rid of illusion is illusion. Just be awake." There is no need to get rid of it.

Illusion is just writing in the air, soap bubbles.

When there is not a hair's breadth of
something to rely on, this is called
"Giving away with both hands,
and thus receiving buddhahood."

This is a Zen expression: giving with both hands means giving totally, not half-heartedly. Your two hands represent your totality. Your mind is divided into two parts. The right hand represents your left mind, the left hand represents your right mind. Crosswise, they are connected.

So it is a symbol of totality: giving with both hands – keeping nothing back, holding nothing. And a man who can give himself to existence with both hands, awakes, becomes a buddha himself.

Giving away with both hands
and thus receiving buddhahood.

Don't be deceived by language. It is the poverty of language that words have to be used which cannot be correct. Receiving buddhahood…the word receiving is not right because buddhahood does not come from somewhere else.

If I was in place of Obaku, I would say, "Open both your hands and you are the buddha." Your clinging, your greed, your holding is the only problem. Just be as open as the sky and buddhahood blossoms in your being.

Haikyu said, "There being nothing to rely on,
how can anything be transmitted?"

He seems to be of a philosophical mind. His questions are logical but Zen or existence or being are simply there, without any logic. He is asking,

"There being nothing to rely on,
how can anything be transmitted?"

Obaku said, "Mind…" with a capital M – the translation should be, 'Consciousness is transmitted by consciousness'. That's what he means by writing Mind with a capital M. When there is silence and no small mind, no thinking, no thought, when there is open space, suddenly two open spaces become one without any effort. There is no way to keep them separate. Can you keep two open spaces separate?

Haikyu said, "If the Mind is transmitted,
why do you say there is no such thing as Mind?"

Haikyu does not understand the difference between a mind with a small m and Mind with a capital M. And the translator does not understand either that for the capital M Mind something else should be used: consciousness, awareness, watchfulness. But the same word creates unnecessary confusion. There is no such thing as the small mind. It is just dust gathered on the mirror. Just clean the mirror and the mirror starts reflecting all the stars and the moon in the sky.

What are your thoughts except dust? Every evening we try to dust off as much as possible because we have been gathering dust for centuries, for many lives. Thick layers are sitting upon our consciousness and anyway, if you don't dust the mirror every day, it will be covered with dust. As time passes dust gathers again. You have to clean your mirror every day. And as far as your consciousness is concerned, you have to cleanse it every moment. Don't allow any thought to settle in your consciousness. Every thought corrupts. Be without any thinking, just a pure opening, a clarity. That is what is meant by meditation.

Obaku said, "Not receiving the law is called
'transmission of Mind'. If you understand what
this Mind is, this is the No-Mind, the No-Law."

It is difficult to understand the language because it is the very special language of Zen. If you are aware, there is no mind and there is no dharma, there is no religion either. You are drowned in the music of the cosmos. Your heartbeat becomes part of the universal heartbeat.

But poor Haikyu seems to be stuck with his logical mind. He says, *"If there is no Mind, and no Law, how can you talk about 'transmitting' something?"* He goes on insisting again and again; he seems to be absolutely incapable of going beyond logic.

Obaku said, "When you hear me say 'transmission of Mind,' you think of there being a 'something' to transmit."

Transmitting consciousness is neither transmitting nor giving, it is just a way to say something which is not available to language. I can look into your eyes and this is transmission. In this silence, I am giving you with both my hands your buddhahood. I am not giving anything but only waking you up.

I'm reminded of a small, but very beautiful story.

One morning when Chuang Tzu woke up, his disciples were very sad because they saw him weeping. They had never seen him even being sad. Tears? Something really bad must have happened.

They asked, "What is the matter? How can we help you?"

Chuang Tzu said, "I don't think you can help me. I have got into trouble. But if you think you can do something I will tell you. Just a few minutes ago I was asleep and in my sleep I saw I had become a butterfly."

The disciples started laughing. They said, "A dream? Becoming a butterfly in a dream...? And you are making so much fuss about it. You, one of the greatest masters!"

Chuang Tzu said, "You have not understood. The problem is not so simple. The problem is that if Chuang Tzu in his dream can become a butterfly, why cannot a butterfly become Chuang Tzu in her dream? Now the problem is, who am I? Chuang Tzu or the butterfly?"

The disciples became aware that this was certainly a difficult problem. They started dispersing outside the hut. "There is no point in staying here because this man is crazy. But his question is right. If Chuang Tzu can become a butterfly, then certainly there is no barrier to a butterfly having a good afternoon nap and becoming Chuang Tzu."

His chief disciple, Lieh Tzu, was out. When he came back, he saw the other disciples sitting sadly outside the hut of Chuang Tzu. They said, "We were waiting for you. Our master is in difficulty and we cannot help. Perhaps you may be able to do something."

He said, "What is the problem?"

They told him the problem. He said, "I'll come."

They said, "Where are you going? The master is inside."

He said, "I'm going to the well."

They said, "This seems strange; the master is suffering and in tears."

Chuang Tzu was waiting for Lieh Tzu: perhaps he would solve the problem; he did solve it. He went to the well – it was wintertime and the water was cold – brought a bucket full of water and poured it over Chuang Tzu. And Chuang Tzu said, "Wait, wait. I am Chuang Tzu, wait."

He said, "Just get right out of the bed. Otherwise I will have to bring another bucket of water – ice-cold. I just went out for a while and you started torturing the other disciples. Ask me the question."

Chuang Tzu said, "There is no question; just take that bucket out. The butterfly has gone. The water is too cold."

All that you need is cold water thrown into your eyes. Nothing has to be transmitted; you just have to be awakened.

When you realize the nature of ultimate *Mind,* the very consciousness of existence, you *speak of it as a wonderful mystery,* not as a problem.

Enlightenment is unattainable.
When attained, you do not describe it
as something known.

Enlightenment is unattainable because you are already enlightened. You have just forgotten it. It is not a question of attaining it, but of remembering it. And when you remember it, you don't have to say anything about it, because anything said is bound to be wrong. No word can contain your spirituality; no word can contain your inner light; no word can contain your immortality.

Obaku said, "If I get you to understand this,
do you think you could?"

I'm also asking the same question to you all. Can you drop the idea of attainment and just be? Can you forget any effort to attain, to know, to inquire and just be a luminous being? Then you will have found the indescribable, the mysterious, the very truth of your existence, the meaning and the significance.

Basho wrote a poem about this dialogue:
Separated we shall be
For ever, my friends,
Like the wild geese
Lost in the clouds.

Basho is saying that if you think with the mind and logic...we shall be separated from our own being and from the being of existence, which are not two things. A dew drop has in it the whole ocean.

Another master, Dogen, wrote about the previous dialogue:

Four and fifty years
I have hung the sky with stars.
Now I leap through –
What shattering!

He is saying, "I have been decorating my mind for fifty years and now I know that I'm not the mind: what shattering, but also what freedom!"

Another master, Shunoku:

After the spring song,
'Vast emptiness, no holiness,'
Comes the song of snow-wind
along the Yangtze river.
Late at night I too play the noteless flute
of Shorin,
Piercing the mountains with its sound,
the river.

Maneesha is asking:

Beloved Bhagwan,
Is nothing *all we can rely on?*

Maneesha, there is no need to rely on anything because you are all. In the ultimate sense all and nothing are synonymous. The day you become awakened you will know: nothing and all are two names of the same experience. Positively you can say, "I am all." Negatively you can say, "I am nothing." But you are both because they are not two.

This is the ultimate experience, brought into language. It is difficult to bring it into language but in silence it comes very easily, without making even the sound of footsteps. In silence it comes, without any whispering.

Before we enter this silence where you are all and nothing, the bamboos are waiting in silence for a few jokes. Too much silence...the poor bamboos remain for twenty-four hours waiting for you, hoping that Sardar Gurudayal Singh will be coming, and he comes.

Two Southern red-necks and Kowalski are removed from a Mississippi courtroom after being sentenced.

In the prison truck one red-neck turns to the other and asks, "What did yarl git?"

"Two goddam years for beating a Polack," the first red-neck groans, "but," he adds more cheerfully, "I will be out in six months with good behavior. What did yarl git?"

"Three goddam years for beating an entire Polack family. But I will be out in ten months with good behavior," says the second red-neck.

After a short silence, they both turn to Kowalski and ask what he got.

"Life," replies Kowalski. "I got life for riding my bike without lights. But," Kowalski brightens, "I should be out in fifteen years. It was not even dark."

Sarjano goes to see Dr. Azima in the medical center. "Doctor," says Sarjano, "I think-a I got-a flying crabs!"

Azima is amazed and takes a test. Sarjano anxiously awaits the results. He is dismayed to see Azima come back with a sad look on his face. "I am-a sorry, Sarjano," says Azima, "but I have-a some good news and-a some bad news."

"Give-a me the good news," replies Sarjano.

"The good-a news," says Azima, "is-a that those flying crabs you-a had, turned out to be-a fruit flies."

"Great-a!" cries Sarjano, "and what about the bad news?"

"I am sorry," says Azima, "but the bad-a news is, your banana is-a dead!"

Ma Papaya Pineapple is standing naked on the floor, talking endlessly. Swami Deva Coconut is lying naked at her feet.

"My life is empty!" cries Papaya Pineapple. "It is a mockery…I am nothing, just a façade, a shell – a dead and useless thing! I am twenty-six years old, and I have never had a meaningful relationship, never had a truly meaningful relationship. I should not admit that, I suppose. It is very humiliating! I have passed from one shallow sexual episode to another. That is the story of my entire life, one shallow clutching incident after another. My relationships have no deep, lasting significance. If I could just once lie down and have something meaningful happen!"

Coconut replies, from the floor, "Have you ever tried talking less, and lying down sooner?"

Two shrinks, Dr. Slope and Dr. Feelgood, are discussing a patient.

"I was having great success with Mr. Philpott," says Slope. "When he first came to me, he was suffering from a massive inferiority complex. He thought that he was too small – which, of course, was all nonsense."

"So how did you treat him?" asks Feelgood.

"I started out with intensive analysis," replies

Slope. "Then I moved him on to group therapy. I convinced him that many of the world's greatest leaders were men of small physical stature. It was a pity; I really hated losing Mr. Philpott."

"What do you mean?" enquires Feelgood. "How did you lose him?"

"A terrible accident – a tragedy!" replies Slope. "The cat ate him!"

Now, Rupesh give the drum for everybody to go crazy.

Rupesh…

Everyone becomes silent.
Close your eyes.
No movement,
just go within.
This is the only temple.
A jump, a quantum leap
from mind to no-mind…
In this silence you are the buddha.
In this silence
opens the lotus of your being.
Deeper and deeper.
Don't be afraid,
you are going into yourself.
There is no question of being afraid.
Fearlessly penetrate to the
deepest core.

To help them, Rupesh, give the beat and everyone dies completely.

Let the body breathe
but you simply become the center
of your innermost being.
This is the truth,
this is the most blissful moment.
Carry this taste
as an undercurrent twenty-four hours
like a fragrance surrounding you.
In every one of your actions
let this silence penetrate
and make them graceful.

Rupesh…

Come back to life,
absolutely new as if you are just born,
fresh, knowing nothing,
with open hands.
You have completed the pilgrimage
from animal to the ultimate consciousness
of being a buddha,
an awakened one.

Okay, Maneesha?
Yes, Bhagwan.
Can we celebrate so many buddhas together?
YES!

Books by
Bhagwan Shree Rajneesh

ENGLISH LANGUAGE EDITIONS

Early Discourses and Writings
A Cup of Tea *Letters to Disciples*
From Sex to Superconsciousnes
I Am the Gate
The Long and the Short and the All
The Silent Explosion

Meditation
And Now, and Here (Volumes 1&2)
The Book of the Secrets (Volumes 1–5) *Vigyana Bhairava Tantra*
Dimensions Beyond the Known
In Search of the Miraculous (Volume 1)
Meditation: the Art of Ecstasy
The Orange Book *The Meditation Techniques of
  Bhagwan Shree Rajneesh*
The Perfect Way
The Psychology of the Esoteric

Buddha and Buddhist Masters
The Book of the Books (Volumes 1–4) *The Dhammapada*
The Diamond Sutra *The Vajrachchedika Prajnaparamita Sutra*
The Discipline of Transcendence (Volumes 1–4)
  On the Sutra of 42 Chapters
The Heart Sutra *The Prajnaparamita Hridayam Sutra*
The Book of Wisdom (Volumes 1&2)
  Atisha's Seven Points of Mind Training

Indian Mystics:
The Bauls
The Beloved (Volumes 1&2)

Kabir
The Divine Melody
Ecstasy – The Forgotten Language
The Fish in the Sea is Not Thirsty
The Guest
The Path of Love
The Revolution

Krishna
Krishna: The Man and His Philosophy

Jesus and Christian Mystics
Come Follow Me (Volumes 1–4) *The Sayings of Jesus*
I Say Unto You (Volumes 1&2) *The Sayings of Jesus*
The Mustard Seed *The Gospel of Thomas*
Theologia Mystica *The Treatise of St. Dionysius*

Jewish Mystics
The Art of Dying
The True Sage

Sufism
Just Like That
The Perfect Master (Volumes 1&2)
The Secret
Sufis: The People of the Path (Volumes 1&2)
Unio Mystica (Volumes 1&2) *The Hadiqa of Hakim Sanai*
Until You Die
The Wisdom of the Sands (Volumes 1&2)

Tantra
Tantra, Spirituality and Sex *Excerpts from The Book of the Secrets*
Tantra: The Supreme Understanding *Tilopa's Song of Mahamudra*
The Tantra Vision (Volumes 1&2) *The Royal Song of Saraha*

Tao
The Empty Boat *The Stories of Chuang Tzu*
The Secret of Secrets (Volumes 1&2)
  The Secret of the Golden Flower
Tao: The Golden Gate (Volumes 1&2)
Tao: The Pathless Path (Volumes 1&2) *The Stories of Lieh Tzu*
Tao: The Three Treasures (Volumes 1–4)
  The Tao Te Ching of Lao Tzu
When the Shoe Fits *The Stories of Chuang Tzu*

The Upanishads
I Am That *Isa Upanishad*
Philosophia Ultima *Mandukya Upanishad*
The Supreme Doctrine *Kenopanishad*
That Art Thou *Sarvasar Upanishad, Kaivalya Upanishad,*
  Adhyatma Upanishad
The Ultimate Alchemy (Volumes 1&2) *Atma Pooja Upanishad*
Vedanta: Seven Steps to Samadhi *Akshya Upanishad*

Western Mystics
Guida Spirituale *On the Desiderata*
The Hidden Harmony
  The Fragments of Heraclitus
The Messiah (Volumes 1&2)
  Commentaries on Kahlil Gibran's The Prophet

The New Alchemy: To Turn You On   *Mabel Collins' Light on the Path*
Philosophia Perennis (Volumes 1&2)
   The Golden Verses of Pythagoras
Zarathustra: A God That Can Dance   *Commentaries on*
   Friedrich Nietzsche's Thus spoke Zarathustra
Zarathustra: The Laughing Prophet   *Commentaries on*
   Friedrich Nietzsche's Thus spoke Zarathustra

Yoga

Yoga: The Alpha and the Omega (Volumes 1–10)
   The Yoga Sutras of Patanjali
Yoga: The Science of the Soul (Volumes 1–3)
   Original title Yoga: The Alpha and the Omega (Volumes 1–3)

Zen and Zen Masters

Ah, This!
Ancient Music in the Pines
And the Flowers Showered
Bodhidharma The Greatest Zen Master   *Commentaries on the*
   Teachings of the Messenger of Zen from India to China
Dang Dang Doko Dang
The First Principle
The Grass Grows By Itself
The Great Zen Master Ta Hui   *Reflections on the Transformation of*
   an Intellectual to Enlightenment
Hsin Hsin Ming: The Book of Nothing
   Discourses on the Faith-Mind of Sosan
Live Zen
Nirvana: The Last Nightmare
No Water, No Moon
Returning to the Source
Roots and Wings
The Search *The Ten Bulls of Zen*
A Sudden Clash of Thunder
The Sun Rises in the Evening
Take it Easy (Volumes 1&2) *Poems of Ikkyu*
This. This. A Thousand Times This.
This Very Body the Buddha *Hakuin's Song of Meditation*
Walking in Zen, Sitting in Zen
The White Lotus   *The Sayings of Bodhidharma*
Zen: The Diamond Thunderbolt
Zen: The Path of Paradox (Volumes 1–3)
Zen: The Quantum Leap from Mind to No-Mind
Zen: The Solitary Bird, Cuckoo of the Forest
Zen: The Special Transmission

Responses to Questions:
Poona 1974-1981
Be Still and Know
The Goose is Out!

My Way: The Way of the White Clouds
Walk Without Feet, Fly Without Wings and
  Think Without Mind
The Wild Geese and the Water
Zen: Zest, Zip, Zap and Zing

Rajneeshpuram
From Darkness to Light *Answers to the Seekers of the Path*
From the False to the Truth *Answers to the Seekers of the Path*
The Rajneesh Bible (Volumes 1–4)

The World Tour
Beyond Psychology *Talks in Uruguay*
Light on the Path *Talks in the Himalayas*
The Path of the Mystic *Talks in Uruguay*
Socrates Poisoned Again After 25 Centuries *Talks in Greece*
The Transmission of the Lamp *Talks in Uruguay*

The Mystery School 1986 – present
Beyond Enlightenment
The Golden Future
The Great Pilgrimage: From Here to Here
Hari Om Tat Sat *The Divine Sound: That is The Truth*
The Hidden Splendor
The Invitation
The New Dawn
Om Mani Padme Hum
  The Sound of Silence: The Diamond in the Lotus
Om Shantih, Shantih, Shantih
  The Soundless Sound: Peace, Peace, Peace
The Rajneesh Upanishad
The Razor's Edge
The Rebellious Spirit
Sat-Chit-Anand *Truth-Consciousness-Bliss*
Satyam-Shivam-Sundram *Truth-Godliness-Beauty*
Sermons in Stones
YAA-HOO! The Mystic Rose

Personal Glimpses
Books I Have Loved
Glimpses of a Golden Childhood
Notes of a Madman

Interviews with the World Press
The Last Testament (Volume 1)

Compilations
Beyond the Frontiers of the Mind
Bhagwan Shree Rajneesh On Basic Human Rights

The Book *An Introduction to theTeachings*
  of Bhagwan Shree Rajneesh
  Series I from A - H
  Series II from I - Q
  Series III from R - Z
Death: The Greatest Fiction
Gold Nuggets
The Greatest Challenge: The Golden Future
I Teach Religiousness Not Religion
Jesus Crucified Again, This Time in Ronald Reagan's America
Life, Love, Laughter
The New Man: The Only Hope for the Future
A New Vision of Women's Liberation
Priests and Politicians: The Mafia of the Soul
The Rebel: The Very Salt of the Earth
Sex: Quotations from Bhagwan Shree Rajneesh

Photobiographies

The Sound of Running Water   *Bhagwan Shree Rajneesh and*
  His Work 1974-1978
This Very Place The Lotus Paradise   *Bhagwan Shree Rajneesh*
  and His Work 1978-1984

Books about Bhagwan Shree Rajneesh

Bhagwan Shree Rajneesh: The Most Dangerous Man
  Since Jesus Christ *(by Sue Appleton, LL.B.)*
Bhagwan: The Buddha For The Future
  (by Juliet Forman, S.R.N., S.C.M., R.M.N.)
Bhagwan: The Most Godless Yet The Most Godly Man
  (by Dr. George Meredith M.D. M.B.,B.S., M.R.C.P.)
Bhagwan: Twelve Days that Shook the World
  (by Juliet Forman, S.R.N., S.C.M., R.M.N.)
Was Bhagwan Shree Rajneesh Poisoned
  by Ronald Reagan's America? *(by Sue Appleton, LL.B.)*

FOREIGN LANGUAGE EDITIONS

Books by Bhagwan Shree Rajneesh have been translated
and published in the following languages:

Chinese	Greek	Marathi	Sindhi
Czech	Gujrati	Nepali	Spanish
Danish	Hebrew	Polish	Swedish
Dutch	Hindi	Portuguese	Tamil
Finnish	Italian	Punjabi	Telugu
French	Japanese	Russian	Urdu
German	Korean	Serbo-Croat	

Worldwide Distribution Centers for the Works of Bhagwan Shree Rajneesh

Books by Bhagwan Shree Rajneesh are available AT COST PRICE in many languages throughout the world. Bhagwan's discourses have been recorded live on audiotape and video-tape. There are many recordings of Rajneesh meditation music and celebration music played in His presence, as well as beautiful photographs of Bhagwan. For further information contact one of the distribution centers below:

EUROPE

Denmark
Anwar Distribution
Carl Johansgade 8, 5
2100 Copenhagen
Tel. 01/420218

Italy
Rajneesh Services Corporation
Via XX Settembre 12
28041 Arona (NO)
Tel. 02/8392 194 (Milan office)

Netherlands
Rajneesh Distributie Centrum
Cornelis Troostplein 23
1072 JJ Amsterdam
Tel. 020/5732 130

Norway
Devananda Rajneesh
Meditation Center
P.O. Box 177 Vinderen
0386 Oslo 3
Tel. 02/123373

Spain
Gulaab Rajneesh Information
and Meditation Center
"Es Serralet"
Estellens
07192 Mallorca - Baleares
Tel. 071/410470

Sweden
Madhur Rajneesh Meditation
Center
Nidalvsgrand 15
12161 Johanneshov
Tel. 08/394996

Switzerland
Mingus AG
Asylstrasse 11
8032 Zurich
Tel. 01/2522 012

United Kingdom
Purnima Rajneesh Publications
Spring House, Spring Place
London NW5 3BH
Tel. 01/ 284 1415

West Germany
The Rebel Publishing
House GmbH
Venloer Strasse 5-7
5000 Cologne 1
Tel. 0221/57407 42

Rajneesh Verlags GmbH
Venloer Strasse 5-7
5000 Cologne 1
Tel. 0221/57407 43

AMERICA

United States
Chidvilas
P.O. Box 17550
Boulder, CO 80308
Tel. 303/665 6611
Order Dept. 800/777 7743

Nartano
P.O. Box 51171
Levittown, Puerto Rico
Tel. 809/795 8829

Also available in bookstores
nationwide at Walden Books
and B. Dalton

AUSTRALIA

Rajneesh Meditation & Healing
Center
P.O. Box 1097
160 High Street
Fremantle, WA 6160
Tel. 09/430 4047

ASIA

India
Sadhana Foundation
17 Koregaon Park
Poona 411 001 M.S.
Tel. 0212/660963

Japan
Eer Rajneesh
Neo-Sannyas Commune
Mimura Building 6-21-34
Kikuna, Kohoku-ku
Yokohama, 222
Tel. 045/434 1981

Rajneesh Meditation Centers Ashrams and Communes

There are many Rajneesh Meditation Centers throughout
the world which can be contacted for information about the
teachings of Bhagwan Shree Rajneesh and which have His
books available as well as audio and video tapes of His
discourses. Centers exist in practically every country.

For further information about Bhagwan Shree Rajneesh

Rajneeshdham Neo-Sannyas Commune
17 Koregaon Park
Poona 411 001, MS
India

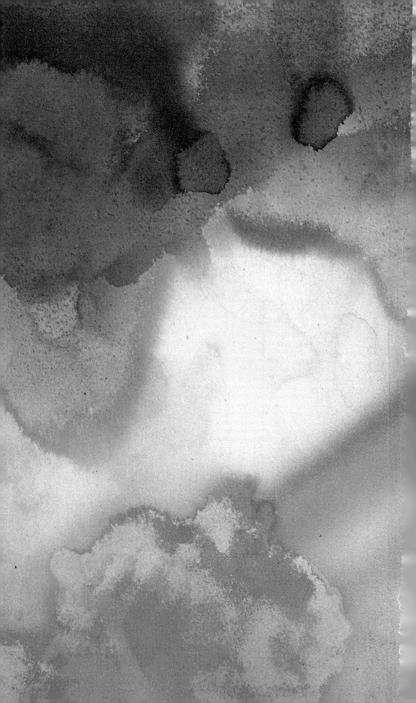